12-14-20

President Carter —
Finally completed
The FLo—ray
Book! I hope
you are doing OK.
— John te—

THE
CONFEDERATE

JOHN W. FLORES

authorHOUSE®

AuthorHouse™
1663 Liberty Drive
Bloomington, IN 47403
www.authorhouse.com
Phone: 833-262-8899

Published by AuthorHouse 11/28/2020

ISBN: 978-1-6655-0820-9 (sc)
ISBN: 978-1-6655-0818-6 (hc)
ISBN: 978-1-6655-0819-3 (e)

Library of Congress Control Number: 2020922889

Print information available on the last page.

"City of the Mardi Gras ... city of a thousand ways of laughter, rich with the romance and tragedy of more than two hundred years of life. It is Carnival Town in the winter, Tropical Port in the summer, and forever an historic monument to the colorful growth and struggle of the people who have lived in it," wrote Harry Devore, in a 1946 book about New Orleans titled simply City of the Mardi Gras. "The old world with its French and Spanish heritage, its quiet courtyards, its wrought-iron gates, its hanging lamps and quaint balustrades ... the new world with its fast, sleek cars, its great buildings rising high above the streets, its giant ships bearing cargoes of food and cloth and steel and a million other things from all the world ... they meet here on the shores of the Mississippi. They are a city of America called New Orleans."

Out of the dark we came, into the dark we go. Like a storm-driven bird at night we fly out of the Nowhere; for a moment our wings are seen in the light of the fire, and, lo! we are gone again into the Nowhere.

~ King Solomon's Mines by H. Rider Haggard

CONTENTS

Introduction xi

Chapter 1   Thunder Across the Plains 1
Chapter 2   Tumblin' Bones 9
Chapter 3   The Gentleman Roughneck 14
Chapter 4   Photographs and Memories 30
Chapter 5   From pyramids to petrol 41
Chapter 6   solid Louisiana boy 52
Chapter 7   Long Years of Wine and Roses 60
Chapter 8   He Knew the Drill All-Right 64
Chapter 9   From whence we were hewn 69
Chapter 10 "Failure is not an option" 85
Chapter 11 Failure is not an option" 93
Chapter 12 The Dean of South Texas Drilling 96
Chapter 13 The pirates of petroleum 107
Chapter 14 A Louisiana man 113
Chapter 15 The Adopted Hometown 117
Chapter 16 Heavy Bomber Pilot Training 119
Chapter 17 A Time to Build 123
Chapter 18 Duty and Courage 137
Chapter 19 Rainbow Luck 142
Chapter 20 Skies of fire 145
Chapter 21 The Key-West Connection 154
Chapter 22 Reverberations 159

Chapter 23   Town on the Move..161
Chapter 24   Time Passengers...163

Bibliography...171
Glossary...173
Index..217

Introduction

MAXINE REMEMBERS: U.S. Senator and Mercury Astronaut John Glenn called, all kinds of powerful people. One day maybe Frank Sinatra, President Jimmy Carter, Bill Clinton, Ted Kennedy, Governor Ann Richards; all the big Democratic people. But those were many years before. She is 99 years of age now. Or was, on March 30, 2020.

About 20 years ago, a strong, tough, smart and good-hearted man, hired me away from my job as a young Albuquerque daily newspaper reporter. Like a commanding general, he had a deep voice, but a high laugh if he really got tickled—and he did have one hell of a sense of humor, something I learned from listening to him, and the many stories about him during my two-year stay there in the oilfield "hub town" of Alice—45 miles west of the vibrant and vital port city of Corpus Christi—home to a giant refinery.

His family name was spelled "Flornoy" in France, where his ancestors lived during the Catholic Church cruelties. As independent-minded people, they rejected the old religion for a new faith, as Protestants, and to start on some great new adventure. Flornoy means a "walnut flower" in Medieval French.

But these were not "wall flower" type people. Maybe tough as nuts.

After some friends and relatives were either tortured and/or killed, that early Flornoy pioneering papa defiantly gathered his belongings and family and they headed for Switzerland, before deciding it might be a good time to venture across the big water of the Atlantic, and see what that new place—a virgin-land called America--was like. His name was Laurent Flornoy, a local jeweler, and he and several other family members and friends—in 1562—managed to make the long trip to America, landing in rich Virginia farm country.

The Flournoy men were known, as a group, as good farmers, and ranchers. They knew how to make honest money, all the way up to a man named Alfred Flournoy, M.D., a veteran of the War of 1812, when he fought in the Battle of Pensacola—as a young soldier under the authority and care of General Andrew Jackson—who had land and a home near the Flournoys.

During a battle "Alfred got a leg blown almost off by a Spanish cannon," Flournoy told me, and I verified it later in documents provided by LSU archives and other Louisiana archives—family interviews, and newspapers, and a few scattered, arcane-but-relevant books on the subject of these early French people in Louisiana.

Alfred Flournoy, M.D.

"The odd thing about it is that Alfred's father did not want his boy, a medical student and (future) doctor to die at 16 on some fool adventure, even if it was for a good cause—keeping the greedy and probably nutty British King out.

Anyway, and this is documented in old family books. He was a direct relative, and I was always proud we were related—separated in time by several decades. General Jackson remembered his solemn pledge to the elder Flournoy—Silas—a wealthy man with a lot of political pull in Tennessee.

Through his Old Man's force of Revolutionary War willpower, Silas would be a great help in making some political connections for the young Alfred.

With one wooden leg. Not even eighteen years of age yet.

"The difficulties failed to deter Alfred. He went back to college and became a physician and surgeon, and took good care of all the folks that were there helping work that big plantation," Mr. Flournoy said.

"Dr. Flournoy was born December 3, 1796, at Farmington Plantation, Virginia, and he died October 29, 1863," Lucien Flournoy told me. "He died in Greenwood. His new home really. He loved the place. But it was a hell of a lotta work. I found that out the tough way, as a boy."

I always called him "sir" automatically. He well-deserved the respect. By most accounts—except for a few people who hated him for various reasons—mostly his success at besting the competition much of the time over a 50-year period.

"Alfred appears to have been removed with his parents from Farmington before he was three years old. Nothing is known of him or his family from 1799 to 1807. Silas willed the plantation to his offspring before he died and he put a special provision in the will: "to free all (slaves) but first make sure they learn a trade so they can take care when we're all gone," Mr. Flournoy said.

A 50-year-old volume of the family history, commissioned for Lucien Flournoy's mother and sisters, states further: "The only personal glimpse we have of the elder Silas Flournoy, was in a letter from his son, to Dr. Alfred Flournoy's own boy ... Alfred Jr. in January of 1852. The young Alfred was in school in McMinville, Tennessee," the story states. Excerpts from the letter, pertaining to Alfred's father read: "It was in opposition of my father's will I went into the Army ... I was determined to gratify my father's heart by performing some distinguished act or valor, to add, in some degree, to the honour of his name. An opportunity offered: most cheerfully did I embrace it.

In the front rank, enveloped in dust and smoke, in a few feet of the enemy's cannon I fell, my left leg carried off by a shot. My military career (he was a lieutenant) was closed. My high hopes at an end. It was then, my son, I had time for reflection. It was then all the advice of my father was remembered, even as I lay surrounded by the dead and maimed. It was long before I returned home. It was the spring of the year, a calm evening in April. I came to my father's home. A high hill overlooked his mansion. I stopped my horse to look. My father had just dismounted from his horse—the children had run out to meet him, my sisters and brothers."

Though at first bitterly disappointed that his son would quit medical school to go fight the British, a second round and seemed foolish to Silas—since his father and other Flournoy relatives fought during the American Revolution.

He wanted his boy, Alfred, to become a surgeon or at least a physician. But Old Man Silas was wise and patient and secretly proud about Alfred. But he did not know how close the boy came to death. Family records show that Alfred was studying medical school at the University of Pennsylvania in summer 1812 and did not return as a student until 1818.

After the grape-shot from that cannon ripped his leg to shreds in that land of Florida—treacherous even in peace time—General Jackson learned that Lt.

Flournoy had been dreadfully wounded, so he summoned the only expert medical help he could find—a nearby British warship, anchored off shore while lounging about licking its wounds from the stinging battle.

According to his obituary, Alfred was caught up with the feverish desire to wipe these British "thieves, drunkards and poltroons" off the face of America forever. So, disobeying his father's direct order, Alfred joined up with the "Tennessee Volunteers" and General Jackson, honoring his pledge to Old Man Flournoy, assigned Alfred to his personal staff.

In March 1812, Jackson issued a call for 50,000 volunteer soldiers—a militia.

According to many sources, including a family genealogist: "In the files of Veterans Administration, OWI, #20367, 'claim for pension' we find ... Alfred Flournoy was commissioned a lieutenant in Major William Butler's Company, the 44th Regiment of the U.S. Infantry, marched from Nashville, Tennessee, to Fort Montgomery, then to Pensacola ..."

The fighting started with the Creek Indians, who were basically British mercenaries in many instances. And Alfred's service as a personal aide on Jackson's staff did not provide the blood rush and excitement of battle that he craved—as many young men will feel. He went around General Jackson, through another officer, and was granted transfer to a front-line battle unit.

On November 7, 1814, the young Flournoy engaged in fierce close warfare near Pensacola—not yet 18 years old.

"He was in the front rank, enveloped in dust and smoke, in a few feet of the enemy's cannon when he fell. He received a Grape Shot in the left leg near the ankle," according to Wayne Spiller, a Flournoy scholar from the 1970s. Mr.

Flournoy provided a stack of books and other material to me, enough that this story had to be cut and heavily edited from a stultifying 650 pages, whittled down to roughly 300—over a period of about five or six years.

Alfred was almost trampled to death by his own cavalry, which charged the enemy soldiers and sailors at the same moment. After the battle, General Jackson took his forces west toward New Orleans, leaving Flournoy behind in his haste. He was reminded of this oversight by an aide.

"He was permanently disabled--the bone of his left leg being shattered …

when the American forces abandoned Pensacola, finally Flournoy was able to be moved near a British fleet that anchored offshore … (at Jackson's urgent and cordial request) and a British officer visited Flournoy and his comrades, and proposed to send his surgeon on shore to examine the wound," according to the war records. "This offer, so humane and generous, was gratefully accepted. The surgeon, after a careful examination, decided it was impossible to save the leg and offered his services to amputate, which was gladly accepted. The operation (one of extreme torture …) was performed in the presence of several other British officers, and during the entire time not a complaint was uttered by Flournoy," according to personal research.

Spiller's research revealed that seven days after Alfred Flournoy's near fatal battle wound, General Jackson wrote to Secretary of State James Monroe: "I have to regret that Alfred Flournoy, acting under my Order as (lieutenant) in Captain W.O. Butler's Company, 44th Infantry, received a severe wound in the leg. He is a brave young man and deserves (a promotion) in the Army."

A month later, on Dec. 24, 1814, Great Britain and the United States signed a peace treaty ending—officially at least—hostilities between the nations. Yet, the Battle of New Orleans was on the horizon and General Jackson knew it.

"The wounded young lieutenant appears to have remained near Pensacola (50 miles east of Mobile) for some two months recuperating from his wound and the consequent surgery. The following letter, dated January 4, 1815, was directed to him at that time:

"Lt. Flournoy: Dear Sir. Isaac Roberts, the bearer of this, takes a horse with the view of bringing you on to this place, he will remain with and attend you on the way. Your most direct way will be to return via Fort Montgomery as you might be a considerable time without our being apprized of it on the opposite side of the Bay. I am extremely happy to find that you are probably able to ride by this time, and hope soon to see you in Mobile. I am very respectfully, sir, your devoted Lieutenant," the letter stated. It was signed by Lt. W.B. Robyon, Aid de Camp. There was a post script: "Col. Perkins and myself send you and Laval fifteen fowls by the party."

The "peace treaty" was shot to tatters on the morning of January 8, 1815,

when the British ships with troops arrived in the New Orleans harbor area, and the British had to leave for home again. This time, Lt. Flournoy would not fight, for by then he was being cared for personally by General Jackson's wife, Rachel, and her nurse maids. Major W.O. Butler accompanied Lt.

Flournoy and Rachel Jackson in a carriage back to Tennessee.

"The last and final stage of the young soldier's journey was probably only a few miles—Nashville to his home nearby," Spiller wrote. Alfred's father's home was located on the south side of the Cumberland near the mouth of Stone's River. The Flournoy plantation cornered on the east bank of Mill Creek, according to (family) deed records. Alfred was on horseback, accompanied by his negro friend, Royal—who worked for the family.

"It was the spring of the year, a calm evening in April," Alfred later wrote.

Overcome with joy and the fear of his father seeing him crippled, he sat on the horse with Royal overlooking his father's mansion. "It was the dark of the evening before I could summon up the fortitude to meet my father. I rode to his gate; he recognized me. He embraced and kissed me. He could not utter a word. Great God, how I felt. I would not again suffer such agony of mind to save my life."

According to his military records: "Lt. Alfred Flournoy was discharged with honorable service on 15 June 1815. He is rated as totally disabled. He shall receive $14 per month (for life) to commence on 16th of June 1815."

He used that money to get back to medical school. He would receive his M.D.

degree on April 15, 1819, and got married to a family friend named Martha Moore a month later. She was 16 years of age.

But married life would not stop Alfred's persistent idea-gazing, and against her orders, which he normally took seriously, in the early spring of 1824, he gathered up some of his property, and property of neighbors who wanted to sell the items, and headed toward Louisiana—on the pretext of doing some trading along the route to New Orleans. Along the way he did trade for 60 mules. He rode by horse and wagon—or carriage. Probably all three modes of transportation. So, evidently, the plantation wasn't doing that well.

By April he was already in New Orleans, the mecca for many people in those days—a glittering city promising leisure and business in equal measure. His tired bones, such that they were, surely welcomed the respite. He would later travel through the old fort city of Natchitoches— still a thriving Central Louisiana township—and on up to Alexandria. With secret dreams of vast cotton fields in his head, on April 23, 1824, Alfred wrote to Martha: "I should leave this place in the morning for the Oppaloosas in order to rest and recruit my mules. It will be necessary for me to remain in that part of the country for six weeks, as it will be that length of time before I shall be able to cross the Mississippi swamp. My mules are in low order and in that time, in such a range, will get fat," he wrote. "My expenses have been enormous, but for the future will be less as I shall camp out altogether. I can scarcely enter a house in this country without paying five or six dollars for it. I wish you to see Mr.

Field. Tell him I am going to return him fifty percent of his money clear of all expenses, unless some *damned* accident should happen to kill some of my mules."

He'd been gone several months, and only received two letters from his lonesome and despondent wife, raising two little boys back home in Tennessee.

So, worried, he wrote her on September 27, 1824: " ... it grieves me much to hear you are so much dissatisfied in your present situation ... the time is now close at hand when I shall return to you. I have had a fatiguing journey so far.

"The greater my hardships are the better health I have. I have escaped so far, and the season is now becoming healthy, but give yourself no concern about me. My life is in the hands of my Maker and he will dispose of me as he pleases. When my hour comes no precaution of mine will avail anything. May the God of Heaven preserve you and my sons from sickness and distress."

After Alfred finally made it back home in the fall of 1824, he learned from a fellow soldier that he could trade in his full pension for government land. He enlisted the aid of all his friends in persuading the U.S. House and Senate to enact a law on May 22, 1826, titled "An Act for the Relief of Alfred Flournoy."

So stated: "Be it enacted that Alfred Flournoy, of the State of Tennessee, lately a lieutenant in the army of the United States, and who, in consequence of the loss of a leg from a Spanish battery at Pensacola, has been placed on the pension list at fourteen dollars a month, be, and he is hereby authorized and empowered, within eighteen months from the passing of this act, to (enter) in any office in the state o Mississippi or Alabama, two sections (about 1,280 acres) of land, in commutation of, and in full discharge of his pension ..."

But he could not get the land he wanted because of red tape, so he called on General Andrew Jackson's friend and colleague, Congressman James K. Polk, who challenged and cut through the Washington road blocks.

After Congress adjourned in early 1827, Rep. Polk wrote to Dr. Flournoy a few weeks later: "I arrived at home yesterday in good health. Some time before the adjournment of Congress, I advised you of the passage of an explanatory law for your relief. Subsequent to that time it received the approval and signature of the President (John Quincy Adams)."

Alfred was the kind of man you could trust at his word—a rare quality throughout human history to be sure. Especially in today's White House and U.S. Senate, and Justice Department. We can only pray in the Lord and mail-in voting, in the meantime. But the Flournoys normally exhibited traits of good breeding—character and honesty in public matters—and it had nothing to do with their status as plantation owners and farmers and education.

Certainly not money. You cannot buy character and honesty as a trait with all the money in the world. Lucien Flournoy, subject of this biography, said: "of all that my good family left me, as an inheritance, the most valued to me are those very character traits. Is it arrogant to brag about being humble? It's arrogant to brag about most things, unless you were World Heavyweight Champion Muhammad Ali—noted as saying 'it ain't braggin' if you can do it.' A great black leader who told the truth with his fists and his poems and his funny observations. We need more honest black and brown people with backbone and brains, and far fewer white political gorillas in our world today, but we keep getting more zoo animals and Neolithics every day— especially in today's government."

There is an engine that powers all those great human qualities—courage fueled by vision—and it seems the Flournoy men and women going back centuries had plenty of horsepower, and good sense, too.

"Uncle Alfred---a great uncle—could have stayed right there at the Tennessee plantation and had it made, as a town doctor. Hell, Andrew Jackson would have made him a governor or something. But he had other ideas, like, he knew there was excellent cotton land down south, in Louisiana, and he intended to ride a horse from Pulaski to the Red River Country of North Louisiana," Lucien told me. "Even with only one leg, but at least it was his left leg—since he was right-handed. I think he was lucky the cannon didn't tear off his right leg. Maybe not. But he did make the ride, and he met with some Caddo tribal people, of the vast Caddo Nation that ran all through northwestern Louisiana, and East Texas—but those lines were not yet drawn into states. It was all just one big wilderness."

Alfred knew how to bullshit, but not as a confidence man, just in the spirit of good will—and the Caddoans knew it at a glance. The Indians sold him hundreds of acres that he would later divide with his family members brave enough to make the long trek from Tennessee.

"I think over again, my small adventures and my fears—those small ones that seemed so big; for all the vital things I had to get and to reach. And yet there is one great thing, the only thing—to live to see the Great Day that dawns and the light that fills the world."

--Old Inuit Song

Chapter 1

THUNDER ACROSS THE PLAINS

The history of crude oil in Louisiana and Texas includes many noteworthy discoveries, *officially* when Spanish conquistadores and explorers in 1543 walked upon tar pits and oil springs in the region, but the first big strike in Texas was in the late 19th century near the city of Corsicana—where the first rotary drill system was used, signaling the rapid decline in the old cable tool "drilling" more ancient and rudimentary than discovery of the wheel.

But even cable tool would be used a few more years.

In 1892, drillers struck oil near Beaumont, too. A lot of oil started pouring in, so, the State of Texas had to develop regulations to govern the growing industry; in 1900 the Powell Field, followed in 1901 by Sour Lake, then the Big Blow in 1901 at Spindletop—a well that changed Texas and the world.

A man named Dad Joiner tapped into an East Texas field so huge it was named "The Black Giant" and not far away in North Louisiana, there was plenty of oil and gas in the big Rodessa Field. Louisiana's oil history is very rich in fact and story, and money too.

When all these giant oceans of subterranean crude were found and tapped, oilfield thinkers—engineers—realized the need for a big pipeline to transport the oil from Texas and Louisiana to the big cities of the east, so "the Big Inch" was welded together and spanned that great distance, and it helped make people in Texas and Louisiana and investors from all over, wealthy even faster. The Big Inch would be a very smart move, indeed.

There were many more big discoveries globally, naturally, since it's a fact that oil circles the globe whether on the surface, a few hundred or tens of thousands of feet below the Earth surface—put there when prehistoric living things died and decayed under layer after layer of mud, rock, salt water, and millions of years passed. Mother Earth just took her time— about 3.8 billion years of organic evolution. Any good geologist can tell you that much—and a lot more.

A Texas oil prospector brought in the state's first producing oil well in 1866, a year after he and financial backers struck oil with a discovery well near a place marked today by a Texas Historical Commission medallion naming the site "Oil Springs".

"At a depth of 106 feet, Lyne Taliaferro Barret brought in the first oil well in Texas in 1866. Well was on a 279-acre lease called the Skillern Tract. On October 9, 1865, Barret, with the financial backing of Charles Hamilton, John B. Earle, Benjamin P. Hollingsworth, and John Flint, formed the Melrose Petroleum Oil Company. Using improvised equipment, this discovery well yielded about 10 barrels per day," according to the marker. "Barret tried unsuccessfully to secure additional financial backing. His venture ultimately failed. He entered the mercantile business, and managed his wife's farm."

THEN CAME SPINDLETOP! That black beauty in 1901 near Houston. And that helped develop Texas war oil. With the legendary Corsicana field.

South Texas oil production started with a successful discovery well on April 21, 1921, between San Antonio and Laredo. The well was drilled by O.W. Killam—a Laredo resident at the time. This well marked the first oilfield between San Antonio and the Rio Grande Valley, and it was one of three wells he would drill in that area—the successes coming one right after the other, continuing for several years. Seven years later he was interviewed and said "I lost count of how many wells I've drilled—whether successful or dry holes— but probably about one hundred, total."

Killam was not an "oilman" when he arrived in South Texas. He said that in the beginning "I didn't know a rotary (rig) from a thrashing machine." He graduated from the University of Missouri and in his earlier life, as a young man, he served as a U.S. Senator in Oklahoma after he worked to help the territory become a state.

"It was just a hunch," Killam said in an old oilfield magazine article, "that me, T.C. Mann, and L.T. Harned came to Laredo late in 1919. We looked things over and decided to stick around about a year until we got our horse-trading done." The three men founded Mirando Oil Company by the end of that year.

Mann and Harned had some oil experience, but Killam did not. Still, he would become their number one oilman because of either luck of good intuition. He said years later that he couldn't remember why he picked those sites to drill wells. He had a plan, in any case, and hired a Mexia (Texas) driller he liked, had lumber for the wooden rig derricks hauled from Laredo, and obtained a 45-horsepower boiler to power the rotary drill. The fuel he used was Mesquite wood—found all over South Texas—with some coal from an old Laredo coal mine. This provided fuel for the first three "wildcat" rigs.

Killam said his wells were never more than about 2,000 feet deep—very shallow by today's standards. But they produced petroleum. The only problem at the time was finding a market for the crude oil—he had to create a demand for it and he had to build refineries, and make pipelines, and finally he was able to get big money boys to buy his product. His first big sale was to Magnolia Petroleum. This was the beginning of what would become a highly successful century of oil and gas drilling throughout South Texas and the Rio Grande Valley.

The first petroleum in Texas was discovered untold centuries ago by Native Americans, but that was just surface oil they'd use for various good reasons. About 20 years after Killam's discovery wells, a young man named Lucien Flournoy had to quit Louisiana State University as a petroleum engineering major—in his third year—due to the Great Depression and the harsh reality that he had no money left for school. So, he started working as a roughneck throughout South Louisiana—from New Orleans to Baton Rouge, up to Natchitoches. In those days, jobs of any kind were hard to find, especially a good-paying position. Back in the 1930s, roughnecks with experience could make $5 dollars per day, and Lucien learned how to save money from his mother, who ran their 270-acre family farm located at the edge of Greenwood, Louisiana—up in the wooded northwest edge of Louisiana. He worked as a roughneck, but his proficiency and intelligence were so keen that he moved right up the ladder—the derrick ladder—up to the delightfully dangerous (to him) job of night tower-man, working 90-feet off the deck at night connecting-coordinating new pipe to be lowered down into the drill hole. And later he would become tool pusher—a top rig job—all before the age of 21. He would also use a letter requested from his petroleum engineer professor at LSU recommending him for a job in the expanding Corpus Christi area, where he would work as a wooden rig-builder in the rich oilfields west of that Coastal Plains port city near the pool table flat land of Robstown. The rig-builders in those days had to be so strong, tough, and fearless, they were called, "the athletes of the oilfields."

This was Lucien Flournoy as a young man. His harsh times—the beginnings of a man who would become one of the most successful independent oilmen in the United States—not just due to speed, luck, talented crewmen, but also his devotion to those employees, and great concern for their safety. If a man died or was hurt badly, he was there at the hospital or at the family home to console and write a check to cover all expenses—hospital or funeral costs. And when the oil business in Texas went bust in the late 1980s, instead of laying off his loyal workers, he sold the company plane and used that money to keep them on at full salary until things picked up. No one else interviewed for this biography could cite any other oilman, anywhere, who ever had such compassion and loyalty for his people. And that loyalty was reciprocated readily—for decades.

Alice 1947 and modern

Flournoy's "new town" of Alice originated from the defunct community of Collins, three miles east. Around 1880 the San Antonio and Aransas Pass Railway attempted to build a line through Collins, which then had about 2,000 inhabitants. The people did not want to sell their land, so the railroad was moved three miles west and in 1883 a depot carried a wooden plank with the name "Bandana" signifying a town or community of some sort or another. This was also where the Corpus Christi, San Diego and Rio Grande Railroad merged. Soon, the small village was a thriving cattle-shipping site, and it wouldn't be long before a post office was named "Kleberg" to honor Robert Kleberg, a San Jacinto battle veteran. But that was changed to "Alice" who was Kleberg's wife—and the daughter of

King Ranch owners Richard and Henrietta King. So, the town of Alice was officially born when the Alice Post Office opened in 1888—just three years after the King Ranch was officially created, the same year Richard King would die in a San Antonio hospital at age 60 from stomach cancer—after a long stage coach ride from the ranch to San Antonio—and King's favorite hide-out and party place, the historic Menger Hotel.

First, Alice became the largest cattle-shipping site in the world during the great cattle era of the latter 19th century, and for years was a major shipping point for area ranchers until petroleum was discovered in and around Alice in the early 20th century, and drilling started big-time in the 1940s, drawing in a lot more people to join the booming population.

Alice was also where U.S. Congressman Lyndon B. Johnson won the Democratic Primary in a race to replace retiring Senator W. Lee "Pappy" O'Daniel. The Congressman won by the 202 ballots in Ballot Box 13, said to have been the names of dead people from a local cemetery alphabetized on orders from "The Duke of Duval" otherwise known as George Parr, a powerful Democrat and patron figure for many poor Mexicans living and working in the Alice-San Diego area.

But that accusation made by jealous and corrupt Republicans and their media darlings in Texas and elsewhere, made up their minds that Parr stole the election for LBJ, and they just couldn't accept it, so they trumped-up some charges against Parr unrelated to the Ballot Box, and in the interim, Parr was almost shot and killed by an angry Republican-leaning Texas Ranger one day in the middle of the Jim Wells County Courthouse. The Ranger would have shot Parr had it not been for Caro Brown, an Alice resident and local newspaper reporter. Her coverage of that event, and the Box 13 incident, earned her the Pulitzer Prize. To date, it is the only Pulitzer the old Alice Echo-News has received. Not many small newspapers get that honor.

LBJ would win handily over Republican candidate Jack Porter, in the Nov. 2, 1948 general election. LBJ had 702,985 votes, and Porter had 349,665 votes.

But the history books still try to make LBJ look like a crook. Republicans write the history books, in many cases.

It is also the town where local Sheriff's Department Deputy Sam Smithwick would, on Jan. 29, 1949, gun down veteran radio announcer and former New York Times reporter Bill Mason, 51, in the middle of the street, downtown, in the middle of the day, over comments he made on-air that angered some local mob types involved in prostitution, drugs, extortion, and murder.

Mason worked for the small Alice station KBKI, and was known to stand up for the "average Joe" and talked for the people who had no voice. He was well-liked, even loved, by many local residents.

Mason said on-air before Smithwick shot him in the chest that he'd been threatened by persons unknown, but South Texas was the Wild West in those days—a lot of cattle, horses, cowboys, mixed with roughnecks, oil, big money and corrupt politicians. Smithwick was sentenced to life in Huntsville State Prison for the murder, and committed suicide in his cell. Mason's epitaph reads: "He Had the Nerve to Tell the Truth for a lot of Little People."

Mason had reported on the Ballot Box 13 situation, and so had a lot of other people—from all over Texas and the United States. The rigged journalistic jury was upended when a judge stepped forward in the summer of 1977 and admitted to a New York Times reporter that he was the one who stuffed that Box 13, though he crawfished and said Parr had ordered him to do it. Parr sometimes chuckled about it, always denying having ordered such a thing. LBJ and his campaign manager, future Texas governor John Connolly, both said the charges made mostly by the right-wingers who hated LBJ and Parr, were either "a flat lie" or "preposterous." LBJ was later cleared by the U.S. Supreme Court. Alice: a lively and colorful town indeed.

"And my story would never be complete, this biography you are writing about me, without the Bob Bullock incident," Flournoy said, turning circles in his office chair as he talked and fiddled with an old black wooden pipe that was much more pleasant smelling than even the best cigars. "I don't light this anymore, by the way. Doctor said I have emphysema, so I can't do that."

The Bullock incident happened back in the early 1970s, when Bullock was an advisor for a big-shot governor—one of the wealthiest Texans. He sent Bullock down to Alice with a request that Flournoy look over a rancher located near Alice, and give his approval for the governor to appoint the white rancher to the Texas Public Safety Commission—overseeing law enforcement in Texas, especially the Texas Department of Public Safety—consisting of Texas Rangers, highway patrol officers, crime lab personnel, and State Capitol security.

"Bullock came in and we shook hands and he said the governor would be very happy if I could recommend that rancher for the commission—a very important and prestigious commission, too. I happened to know that the rancher, who I will not name, had murdered an illegal Mexican worker on his ranch and buried him there. So, I told Bullock that I refused to consider the man for that position. Bullock—future Comptroller and Lieutenant Governor—was not too happy. He went to that rancher and told him about my decision, and pretty soon after that I found out through my security man that the rancher concerned here had put out a "hit" on me for blocking him.

"I called him up and said, 'I'm here and I'm not going anywhere.' He knew I meant business, so he backed off, and that's why every time I drive past the State of Texas' Bob Bullock Museum I want to vomit."

Chapter 2

TUMBLIN' BONES

God was usually pretty decent to young Lucien Flournoy and probably for a good reason, but in the late 1990s at the age of 80, Flournoy had just sold his drilling company for about $50 million and still ran the highly lucrative and somewhat complex-nebulous Flournoy Production Company with headquarters in a modest old former city utilities building at 1909 East Main Street, on the eastern edge of town. He would sit behind his modest office desk restlessly at times, doodling around while he whistled some tune or another, thinking. Some people whistle to help them think. Flournoy whistled, wriggled in the captain's chair--similar to that of the admiral of an aircraft carrier. The chair was covered with black leather and it rose, high and wide above and beside this big man with the deep voice and calmness all about him. And he would telephone. Relentlessly. Always looking, thinking, wondering, pondering. Calculating.

The office in Alice was always quiet, like a church, and every once-in-a-while you might hear the heavy noise of a big oilfield truck pass by the highway, but not having Flournoy around much became a real problem and a worry. Then he would finally show-up again with his assistants and we would be at it again.

"At the risk of repeating myself, did you know, my boy, my best subject in college at LSU was differential calculus? Well, it was. I made top marks all through the time I was there, while working as a butcher, and about every job they had on campus, just to stay in school.

"My father died from the flu epidemic of 1918, after pulling one of his cows out of a cold, muddy ditch just down the road from our home place. That was in the winter of 1918, and about a million Americans died of the flu that year, and fifty million worldwide died. There was no penicillin for bacterial infections in those days—that wouldn't come until just after World War II for wide use among civilians. And the flu virus had no remedy either. So, people just flat out DIED," he said, his dark blue eyes glistening as he intensely gazed ahead, looking to the side, and his eyebrows raising slightly to emphasize his point.

He never really liked to dwell on the negative, and quickly changed the topic.

"I had a mathematics professor and we called him "Colonel Cole" and he was in World War I, and as a young cadet in about 1905, at LSU, he got into trouble many times and had to march around the flag pole many times. He got sick of it and procured some dynamite and blew the flag pole down. He got in even more trouble. Later, years later, he was a distinguished professor.

"One thing we did. We must have been about 12 years old, we walked to school, walking home for daily lunch," Flournoy said, slapping my knee with a diamond-studded pinkie.

"We decided on April Fool's Day were going to walk over and inspect the colored school. The teacher was a friend of our family, and we knew a lot of the pupils, so we went in and sat in the back row. Didn't say a word, the black kids started giggling, the teacher then decided the best way for her to handle this situation— "STUDENTS, WE'RE HAVIN' RECESS EARLY TODAY!"

The best words practically any kid can hear.

Flournoy said he and his buddies laughed about that, the black friends too.

"We thought we might get into trouble. But we had a different kind of situation there in Greenwood. The first integration, you might say," he said with a soft chuckle.

The Flournoys were good people with intellect and muscles to put ideas into action. To them, blacks were the same as whites in the eyes of the Great Spirit who made everything. And that pandemic had a powerful effect, too. When everybody's suffering, everybody has to pull together whether white, black, brown, yellow, orange or purple polka-dotted.

A man named John Coltrane, M.D., made a startling observation during the 1918 pandemic: "Nothing to treat it with. Doctors here were helpless among the clouds of death, watching from fence posts peering upon the stench like festering vultures."

Flournoy said that terrible flu brought the community together spiritually, though not physically: "It really did. We didn't have too many people, but we learned that the best way to handle tough times is to endeavor to endure. And we did, too. We somehow made it. Many people did not."

The pandemic erupted right after the Great War took 50 million lives at least--and that flu bug was the first identified in service personnel. So those soldiers sometimes got the shaft, both ways. And in those days the world was not all that populated, so 500 million infected--still just a rough estimate--was a lot of people on Earth.

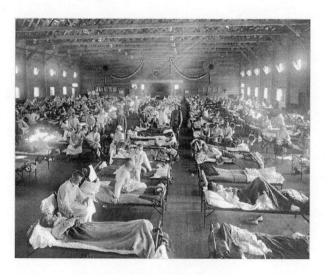

1918 flu victims in Kansas

The 1918 flu infected 225,857 Louisiana residents, out of a statewide population of 1,750,000. About five thousand (Louisiana) people died from the flu that year.

Lucien Flournoy Sr. was in his 40s, handsome, strong as a buffalo, and probably abut as stubborn if he was anything like his son would become. But even he could not beat old age and disease.

Mortality was high in people younger than 5 years old, and 65 years and older. The high mortality in healthy people, including those in the 20-40-year age group, was a unique feature of this 1918 pandemic.

The Nuclear Flu (COVID-19) in 2020 is spread like the flu of 1918. Normal flu treatment was ineffective, and the COVID-19 virus spread began to increase exponentially across most of the United States through fall 2020. Spread control efforts still included isolation, quarantine, good personal hygiene, and other common-sense efforts.

Paradoxically, medical advancements—many, like widespread penicillin—came about from the aftermath of the catastrophic Second World War. Even the space program got its real start under German Nazi Scientist Wernher von Braun. Like the oil business, or anything else, everything has good points and bad ones. Sometimes brutal beginnings lead to great glories.

Penicillin still would have helped save his relatives, and Flournoy remembered that many people were saved from various bacterial infections when the drug was finally widely available by 1943 in Caddo Parish.

A March 14, 1942 newspaper story detailed the remarkable medical achievement titled in bold letters: FIRST AMERICAN TREATED WITH PENICILLIN: By Jenny Ashcraft--"on March 14, 1942, Ann Miller, 33, nearly died in a Connecticut hospital, suffering for weeks with a high fever. She developed septicemia, or blood poisoning, after a miscarriage. Doctors tried every known treatment, and in a last-ditch effort to save her life tried a new drug called penicillin. The government released nearly half of its entire supply. Within a day, Anne's temperature returned to normal and she was on the road to recovery. Anne became the first American treated with penicillin. This newly developed miracle drug would ultimately save the lives of millions, including countless soldiers during WWII.

Penicillin, Miracle Drug, Soon Out In Patent Forms; But Best See Doctor First

NOBEL PRIZE TO 3 FOR PENICILLIN DISCOVERY

Stockholm, Oct. 26 — Sir Alexander Fleming of London University, discovered of penicillin, together with two of his co-workers in penicillin research, were awarded the 1945 Nobel Prize for physiology and medicine, it was officially announced Thursday.

Jointly receiving the award with Sir Alexander were Dr. Ernest Boris Chain and Sir Howard Walter Flory, both of Oxford.

Dr. Chain, a German political refugee, who went to England in 1938, is professor of chemical pathology at the William Dunn School of Pathology, Oxford.

Penicillin Saves Life of Soldier 'Good as Dead'

BY FRANK CAREY
Associated Press Science Writer

WASHINGTON, Jan. 15. — A new page in the glowing record of penicillin was written today when Army doctors credited the drug with saving the life of a soldier afflicted with a brain disorder always considered a certain killer.

CHAPTER 3

THE GENTLEMAN ROUGHNECK

Flournoy often would raise his eyebrows when making a point, or if he said something to try and shock you. And he liked to shock people sometimes— with ribald jokes, not particularly dirty, but often very funny. Or wild stories of his youth growing up on the family farm, or harrowing oilfield experiences, of one kind or another—rigs blowing up, men being killed or maimed, oilfield fires in South Texas near Alice that would burn for days or even weeks before an expert like the legendary Red Adair could arrive and put the fire out using high explosives to blow all the oxygen away from the flame for a couple of seconds—long enough to hit the affected rig with foam or water, or whatever else was effective enough to put out the fire.

And when Flournoy sometimes would laugh, his eyebrows would raise in a different way, obliquely upward at the top to convey instantly his amusement, along with a ready smile and a muffled chuckle or two. He was not a phony—not a phony bone in his body—and he did not pretend. He was often very direct, but also diplomatic when necessary. And he had a very big heart all his life—rich or poor, good times or bad times. He never forgot the pain of that Great Depression and the absence of a father in his home.

"My dad died a few months before I was born in May of 1919," he said. "My mother, Lillie May, already had four daughters with my father, and then I came along as the baby, *I guess you could say*, of the family. My sisters were my real teachers, too. They were all college grads, well-educated and taught me all kinds of subjects, including how to play classical music

14

on our piano at home. We were not wealthy at all, but we had the farm, raised cotton on good land, and had a dairy, so we did alright. We did fine," Flournoy said.

"I remember the deep-set eyes of hungry, desperate people during the Depression as they stood at our doorway and my mother would give them something to eat before they shambled on down the road. I never forgot the desperation, the misery, in their voices and eyes. It was like watching "The Grapes of Wrath" in real life. Real human beings, dying from starvation and disease. My mother would always give whatever she could, because those people were starving. She was a strong, and a good woman. She taught me how to be a good businessman, I think. I think that's where I learned my business sense and how to save money, working the dairy and selling milk and eggs in town, and helping her run the farm. And we hired hands to help us out, too. Many were people we knew from nearby."

Flournoy hired me to write his biography in the summer of 2001, and I spent a couple of years working on research and writing, until about the time he died from a heart attack in March 2003, and then my wife and I returned to Albuquerque, New Mexico, where I'd been working as a staff writer for the statewide daily newspaper—the Albuquerque Journal.

U.S. Sen. Huey Long

He told me during one of our many interview bull sessions—often more bull than interview—that at LSU his first roommate was a college football phenomenon named Young Bussey—heavily recruiting personally by U.S. Senator Huey Long, a powerful Louisiana politician who loved few things in life more than the LSU Tigers football team. And he made sure all Tigers always had the best of everything—as Louisiana governor and later, as a powerfully persuasive U.S. Senator.

Young Bussey '40

Bears including Young Bussey

"Bussey was my roommate for a couple of years, so we became very good buddies in that time. He was the big man on campus. I had maybe one decent suit, and a few clothes, and a cardboard *pray it don't rain* suitcase, but when I arrived at the stadium dorms, and started to put my clothes in the closet, there was not much room because Bussey had enough clothes and suits for two closets. One of the perks of being the star running back for LSU was that Long made sure Bussey had whatever he asked for—within reason I suppose. When asked by Long what it would take to land him, Bussey said he wanted full rides (scholarships) for a brother, and his "agent" who was just a high school buddy, and he said he'd read that Clark Gable had 100 suits. He told Long, `you give me 101 suits and you got a deal'. They shook on it. And sure enough, he got the suits. And he let me wear them whenever I wanted, so we were the two best-dressed young men on campus—besides Huey Long's son, Russell. We were all three about the same age and Russell liked Young, too, so we all became good buddies," Flournoy said.

Russell Long would later become a powerful U.S. Senator from Louisiana. He did a great deal to help Louisiana citizens but in college he was pale and skinny, but lively and sociable.

While working for Flournoy, I found a book about Young Bussey titled

"Young Bussey—Young Stud" by Texas author Ralph Cushman, published in the early 1990s, and he read it for the first time. Flournoy hadn't seen any part of his LSU student life in print ever before, and found out a lot about his former buddy who went on to be a star with the Chicago Bears during their 1941 championship season.

LSU Dorm

After graduating from LSU with a degree in engineering, Bussey was recruited by legendary Chicago Bears Head Coach George Halas, who found Bussey unruly and bossy, but very dedicated and talented. And tough as hell. When Pearl Harbor was bombed, and like so many other Americans, Bussey joined up in the military immediately to do his duty for America. Halas was furious. He told Bussey not to go—he had a great career in professional football ahead of him. But Bussey would not listen, and he went to the Philippines as a Navy officer, and was killed by a Japanese surprise attack as his patrol boat approached a beach. His body was never found, but "his mother in Houston kept the front porch light on every night for years hoping he would find his way home," Flournoy said, with tears forming as he turned the chair and gazed out the office window at a young black-and-tan German Shepherd trotting past on the street, panting heavily in that first hot, humid morning of my job working on Flournoy's life story. Already Flournoy was forcefully arguing with anybody who would listen, even if they agreed, about "the Dubya problem" since it'd been—after all—almost six months since George W.

Bush assumed the presidency. After his morning "rounds" were done that day, Flournoy called me in to his office—he just yelled out to me, sitting in the lobby near an assistant's desk. He'd kicked me out of his office into the hall, so he could make the calls, and an hour later, there I was again—with notepad and pen, and he picked right up where we'd left off. He was definitely in the mood to talk—and he was quite a garrulous man and when animated with stories about his life, work, or politics, or whatever else moved him, the years on his face vanished. He was a young buck again, and you could see that. Not that he was desperate to be a kid again. He was happy with his life, what he'd accomplished, and didn't regret much. That would be a waste of his time—and he did not like wasting anything unless he could afford it. Time, in the summer of 2001, was something he could not afford.

"I cried and I laughed when I read that book," Flournoy told me, later. "We had some great times as young men at LSU, for those three years. Bussey went on to graduate as an engineer. There were four of us who were best friends, and we would always go to Mardi Gras in New Orleans with what little money we had. After I left LSU in 1939, we agreed to all meet at the Roosevelt Hotel on Canal Street—now it's a big chain hotel but still there—and we'd hit the French Quarter. We had one helluva time, and sometimes got into brawls, but Bussey would be able to dispatch even the biggest guys, if it came to that. He loved to drink and party and so did I, but then he died, and one by one everybody else did, too.

Channing Stowell

One of my good buddies was Channing Stowell, and he was a bomber pilot some years later and was killed during a test flight over Ohio ... that makes me the last one left out of the four of us," he said, matter-of-factly, with just a drop in his voice but no tears or emotion.

The Associated Press news report of the Air Force B-50 Superfortress crash, piloted by Stowell, was carried by newspapers across the country on Feb. 27, 1956, a day after the tragic event: "A four-engine Superfort carrying 11 crewmen on a brief test flight, crashed and then exploded on a farm near here today, killing all aboard," the AP article stated. "eyewitness accounts indicated the big plane was crippled, and heading for an emergency landing when it crashed. The flaming wreck, after hitting the ground about a quarter of a mile west of the highway, continued on, struck the house and another building, setting them on fire, then went on across the road (Wilmington Pike), scattering wreckage and bits of wreckage and bodies for another quarter of a mile."

The elder Stowell said his son, "a graduate of Louisiana State University, is married and the father of three children. His wife and two of the youngsters are visiting her parents in Baton Rouge, Louisiana," the article stated.

Flournoy didn't show it, but deep inside he said he felt the loss of those three good college buddies deeply—especially touched by Young Bussey's death in a surprise Japanese attack during World War II in the Philippines. Bussey's death may have had a chilling effect on the young Flournoy, and caused him to delay joining the military, at least initially. He hinted at that, anyway, in one of our interviews emphasizing the fact that his oilfield expertise was as vital, or more so, than anything else he could have done against enemy forces.

Flournoy had some luck to go along with his intellect and work ethic. He would join the Army Air Corps, but not right after Pearl Harbor was attacked. At that time, he was working as a petroleum engineer in Bakersfield, California, and preferred to stay on-the-job as an essential worker providing fuel for the war.

Bussey with Bears

"I believed that type of work was just as important as anything, and it was, because without fuel we would have lost the war anyway. But after a while people starting looking at me a little *funny,* and I realized they expected me to go and serve, and so I joined up and after basic training, entered bomber flight school but during training I suffered an injury that sidelined me, and the Army took advantage of my schooling and aptitude in physics and made me a physics instructor! Can you imagine? I wanted to be a bomber pilot.

So, I weathered out the war in that capacity. The injury reignited a boyhood Rheumatoid Arthritis problem that I believe came about when I was a boy and us kids were all jumping up and down on a bed at home, playing, and my left leg hit a needle on the bed and it went in deeply, and later I had to be hospitalized at the Shriner's Hospital nearby. They diagnosed me with the arthritis. The needle hit a nerve; I suppose. The problem never really went away. But it might have saved my life from the horrors of World War II—where I was definitely headed."

He laughed remembering a couple of rambling thoughts of those days: "Yeah, I was so angry with my mother for sending me to that hospital, when she visited, I wouldn't even talk to her for a while. And you know, in those times, we were so poor that I had to play basketball games wearing those slick bottom Sunday dress shoes. Man, I slid all over the court. The crowd laughed, as you can imagine. A poor country boy."

After World War II was over, Flournoy's employer assigned him to work in Alice, not far from where he'd labored on building wooden rigs near Robstown a few years earlier. He drove from Bakersfield, and right away was wondering why he was there in a tiny little backwater Texas town. It was named for the daughter of legendary South Texas ranchers, Richard and Henrietta King—founders of the million-acre King Ranch, one of the largest cattle operations and ranches in the world for as long as he could recall. He couldn't imagine it then, but some years later, Flournoy would drill a thousand wells in and around the Ranch, as a contractor for Exxon. But to him, on arriving in Alice, the future did not seem necessarily all that bright.

"I got a hotel room in town, got my suitcase out of the trunk, threw it on the bed and tossed my car keys down, and sat down and I wondered 'what the hell am I doing here?' He chuckled a little, in slight amusement, remembering his initial feelings of loneliness and a little desperation and uncertainty about this move.

Young Lucien roamed the town with eyes like lanterns, a sailor of the prairie anointed in booze at the midnight hour. He liked people, whether friend or foe. He liked a good argument or fist-fight sometimes just to balance everything out—if things were going a little too good for comfort. Flournoy didn't like too much smooth sailing. He was bored with

22

routine and craved action and adventure and danger, when he could get it. Especially if it made money. And a mountain of it.

Flournoy was indeed a very big man in many important ways. Tough as an old Army mule. Much like his ancestor, Alfred. He was his own man—owned by nobody really, even when working for somebody.

"I want a lot of the best things, for my family and friends—and my town. There's plenty to go around. The message I get is that life is a banquet, and most people are starving themselves to death," he said to me early-on in the work of his life recollections.

As a young man—and until he died, really—Flournoy seemed to fit the 16th century instructions on 'how to be the perfect man.' From Castiglione's *The Courtier*: a fine athlete? Check. A brilliant conversationalist? Check. A superb drinker? Check. In everything sort of a renaissance man. He had a good dose of humility in his personality—from his mother no doubt. But hard-earned **honest** money "made him peacock proud," according to an old Shreveport Times article.

As he worked with his spirit, brains and his muscles to build a life in South Louisiana and later in Texas, he seemed to be enveloped in a golden cloud of intoxication, breathing in heavenly mists—blue-chinned and bleary-eyed.

In those early times, he was remembering the heady, romantic days when he and his new bride, a woman he met who was working in a South Louisiana bar, moved from Louisiana to Bakersfield. She was a true beauty, he said, and they traveled around California and in San Francisco stumbled upon the set of a new movie called "Citizen Kane." It would become one of their favorite movies. Flournoy liked a variety of movies, and some TV dramas, but he had no time for hobbies. Drilling was his work, and his hobby. His passion.

"We were well-dressed, young people, and she was gorgeous, and we were noticed and Orson Welles was there. Some of the film crew invited us to watch the scene they were filming, and they took us on a little tour and introduced us to people. That was interesting," he said. He said it flatly, crisply, lowering his gaze right at me, as if a little contemptuous of anything other than brutally hard work: "movie work is for soft hands and softer heads," he would say.

"But my young bride would later leave while I was at work and not return for a few days, and I finally realized she had a problem. I took her to a doctor and he diagnosed her as a schizophrenic. She was in bad shape, so I had to have her committed to a hospital for treatment," he said, as he reached into his back pocket and pulled out his wallet.

He fumbled through the wallet for a couple of minutes and in the back found what he was looking for and pulled out a photo of the young woman.

Like Maxine, she was a real beauty, as he said she was. And he kept her photograph in the back of his wallet until his death, and he checked up on her and made sure she was always getting proper treatment almost until his end. It was *those* memories that worried him when he arrived in Alice, a single man again and all alone in the middle of the vast Coastal prairie land—millions of open acres, mostly ranch land used for cattle and hunting.

"Her name was Evelyn, and she was a runaway from Saint Louis," he said. "Her own mother put her, and her brother, in a boarding school when she was fifteen or sixteen. I met her in a café and restaurant, and a place to dance, in Plaquemines Parish, Louisiana. She had been with the carnival, traveling with them, and it was in reality probably better for her than the boarding school. We had a lot of happiness together. We lived in Oakland, Los Angeles, Bakersfield. She was a good companion. She loved to drink and smoke, but the job I had was not good for her. I was gone a lot."

Flournoy said a man named Kirkwood introduced him to the woman who would be the mother of his children--Maxine Edmondson in Alice.

"I had vowed I would never marry again because my ex-wife was in the San Antonio nut house. But Maxine and I dated a while, so I had to go up to see Evelyn but she didn't have any idea what I was talking about so I had the marriage annulled after we'd been separated. I couldn't figure out why she would always just disappear and then show up again. I never could. In 1982, I went up to New York City and tried to buy the sled named Rosebud from the movie, Citizen Kane. I bid $60,000, but was out-bid at the Sotheby's auction by none other than Stephen Spielberg. I set my bid limit at $60,000, and held firm to that kind of discipline, though I seriously wanted (Rosebud).

"I guess I was trying to hang on to some memory of my life with her. At the time I went to New York, Maxine and I were separated. Evelyn had a boyfriend or someone who cared for her in Saint Louis at that time, and she lived in a halfway house … I've been knowing her for 60-plus years, from 1939 to now," Flournoy said. "Back then I had pretty high morals. Real high." He didn't dwell too much on the "old days" because his mind was always moving. Always working. Always wondering how to make things work better, what investments might yield most profit for his effort. That's what made him so good. That was the essence of his drive to succeed. Money and power, to him, were not prime movers at all. That just came with success in drilling for oil and natural gas. He also had a sideline water-well drilling business in Central America, at one time, and it provided clean water for villages and towns. He tried that as a "kind of a lark, really. But water sure was important to those people," he said. "I remember standing up when the plane landed in some Central American city, and I'd had a few drinks so I was pretty well bagged, and I stood up and people were waving at me—I felt like a movie star for a second there and waved right back," he said, breaking out in a chuckle. "Those good people deserved good water, but they thought I was the Second Coming …"

After working in Alice as a petroleum engineer for a year or so, he'd saved up some money (in those days the $1,200 he saved was equal to about $13,000 in 2020) and decided to put a plan into action—the man of ideas and the muscle to make them happen—and developed blueprints for a new type of portable rig that would cut drilling time way down. It was his design, and with the help of the two welders, they built the first rig that he named "bread and butter." He'd bought an old heavy-duty World War II Navy truck at auction on the nearby Naval Air Station Corpus Christi, and used that to haul the rig from site to site. The success was immediate, and he was soon in-demand by people interested in cashing-in on oil beneath the harsh and desolate landscape of the South Texas Plains.

"So, we made a second rig, like the first one, and I named that one "Marmalade", he said, grinning slightly. He whistled a little and doodled on a pad. "After that, money starting coming in and I decided to start my own company. Later it would be known as Flournoy Drilling, and we had many rigs operating."

Flournoy developed that first rig in 1946-47, about the time he married the young and brave Mary Maxine Edmondson, from Joplin, Missouri.

She'd been flying for the WASPs—Women Airforce Service Pilots—flying Army Air Corps planes as a kind of test pilot in the continental U.S. After the war, she was hired to fly for an oil pipeline company in Houston, with an office in Alice. That's how Flournoy met Maxine. They were young, attractive, dynamic, and lived life boldly, with a sense of daring and style.

Mary Maxine Edmondson

He was attracted to her beauty, personality, and intellect, as one of the few women at that time flying professionally—and it took a lot of guts to be a WASP. A dangerous, and fairly often, a fatal duty during the war years.

Maxine was attracted to him because he was roughly nice-looking, carried himself with an alternately humble and cocky demeanor, he was also fun to be with, and had big ideas with the experience to back them. He knew how to treat her like the lady she was. And she would always be a lady, too—though she was as brave and strong as Flournoy.

Plus, for all his wild ways, Flournoy was always a classy man. He dressed well, displayed manners always *in public,* and knew how to get along with people—though he also had a quick temper. Max could see that he was a winner, she would later say. He had common-sense, imagination and harnessed that to hard work—the formula for his success in the oilfields— or for most anyone in any field. He was formidable physically—tall, thin, and strong. But he said the most important of all was his reputation and his natural ability to make peace and gain respect from even his most fierce competitors in the drilling business across Texas and Louisiana.

Lucien and Maxine were married at 5 p.m., on Saturday, June 29, 1946, at the Presbyterian Church in Alice. The honeymoon, Flournoy told me, "was pretty short and sweet ... I was a working man."

According to an article in the Shreveport Times, "in a double-ring ceremony characterized by beauty and simplicity, Miss Maxine Edmondson, daughter of Mrs. Ruth Jones of Rosemead, Calif., exchanged nuptial vows with Lucien Flournoy, son of Mrs. L. Flournoy and the late Lucien Flournoy of Greenwood … the church was decorated with white gladioli and pink peonies with white tapers at each side. Mrs. Barbara Pyle at the organ played a program of nuptial musts, including "Because," "I Love You Truly" and "At Dawning." The bride entered to the strains of the traditional wedding march. She wore a white organdy gown with a white net veil trimmed with seed pearls and carried a purple orchid with white carnations."

Flournoy Working

Flournoy would be throwing up right about here, if he were reading this, but I shall continue, for the sake of scholarship-in-matrimony (a lost art?) and historical accuracy, while illuminating a few important details about the Flournoys and their times: "The bride's attendants were Mrs. Ann M. Dance of Corpus Christi, who served as matron of honor and Miss Louise Stromberg, bridesmaid. Mrs. Dance wore a pink lace and chiffon dress with a circle of flowers in her hair, and carried a pink nosegay of blue bells and pink peonies with ribbon streamers. Miss Stromberg wore a light green net dress with a flower hat and carried a nosegay.

"Boyd McRae of Beeville attended the bridegroom as best man and the usher was Lou Patillo of Corpus Christi. Immediately following the ceremony, a reception was held at the home of Miss Stromberg (where) Mrs. Pyle served the four-tiered wedding cake which was embossed with green and white rosebuds and topped with a miniature bride and groom.

Miss Catherine Stribling presided at the punch bowl," the Times article declared.

Flournoy laughed about a slight problem that happened at their wedding. "Somebody spiked the punch bowl and it was party time for the elderly. They used to call that old home-made stuff *brush whiskey*, about 100-proof. Old ladies were getting a little bit frisky there."

"Mrs. Flournoy attended the University of Missouri and served in the United States Army as a WASP, and at the present time is employed as a pilot for a contractor in Alice, Texas. Mr. Flournoy attended LSU before volunteering for service in the Air Corps (for B-17 pilot training) and at present is employed as a petroleum engineer for a fuel oil company," the article stated.

After living in South Texas apartments for a few years, finally the Flournoys bought a nice big brick home near the eastern edge of Alice, Texas, in the best area of town in the middle of oceans of oil beneath their feet, sloshing away aimlessly as the Earth rotated around the sun, and it was up to men of practical genius and experienced crews to find a way to get there, way down there--where the dark and heat was as black and inscrutable as that crude oil—made, by God and pressure, from decayed organisms hundreds of millions of years ago; the black (sometimes yellow-colored crude) that was turned to mean green dollars in Texas and his home state of Louisiana. But Texas was the largest state with the blackest soil and the whitest people and America was the greatest nation in the world and his kids were Flournoy's sweetest little girls. He and Maxine would raise three daughters; Mary, Betty Lou, and Helen. All three girls went to school in Alice, and to this day live near each other in Corpus Christi.

"She was an excellent mother," Flournoy said of Maxine. "She backed me up, too, and that was vital."

Maxine showed she was a true lady in many ways through her lifetime—and she turned 99 on March 30, 2020—especially in the wake of her husband's infidelities and the boozing hard that caused it. He never drank much before he got wealthy, he was so busy building up his business. But he kind of cut loose after that—for a few years.

"Don't ever go that route boy," he said to me. "That way leads to nothing BUT trouble."

"There are three things in life that are real: God, human folly, and laughter. The first two are beyond our comprehension, so we must do what we can with the third." –President John F. Kennedy

CHAPTER 4

PHOTOGRAPHS AND MEMORIES

Over the course of that summer, and for the next year, Lucien would often sit at his office desk and talk for hours, but only a couple of times a week, because he was suffering from cancer and heart problems and was whisked off to Corpus Christi doctors and hospitals by his bodyguard several times a week. But his stories, a lot of truth and a little fiction, filled up about two dozen of my notebooks and several tape recordings—though like most people, he was not as easy to talk when being taped. Most people are like that.

He would speak in detail about his life growing up with his mother and four sisters on the large farm and dairy there in Caddo Parish, and his best childhood friend filled in some gaps as well. He had his own stories. This man was DeOrsay Simpson, and he lived near the Flournoy Home as a boy, and the two boys were always pranksters, and hot-rodders, it seemed. They had many stories and it was quite a fun childhood growing up in that rural area, near the small town. But their play-time was often interrupted by the necessity of hard work—picking cotton in summers, hauling in hay from the large fields, working on fences that needed some repair to keep the cattle from straying outside the land, getting up early to milk the cows, feeding the chickens, and the cows, and the Flournoy family horse, Old Bob, among many other daily chores.

Flournoy and his four sisters—Lillian May, Mary Wise, Alma Elizabeth, and Laura Louise--would all pitch in to help their widowed mother in various ways, though the girls most often helped around the house with washing clothes, cooking, cleaning, and gardening.

Lillian, born Nov. 23, 1906 in Greenwood, was christened in the Greenwood Methodist Church, and after high school she attended Louisiana State Normal and received a teaching certificate. She taught for a few years in Caspiana, Louisiana, and had two children with her husband, Roger Hammett.

Mary was born Feb. 3, 1911, in Greenwood, and was also christened at the Methodist Church.

"From her very early childhood it seemed obvious to her father that Mary had inherited **his** love for music. When she was five, he bought her a violin," according to family records. "At Hutchinson Brothers, a music and variety store in Shreveport, she was often able to listen to the great recordings of her day, and her love for music grew and developed as a result.

"Devastated and grief-stricken by her father's death when she was only seven, Mary determined that she'd buck-up, stand up, and be a comfort to her mother, and she followed-through with her personal pledge," the family records show. "Even though she had played the piano by ear from childhood, she wanted a formal education in music. Shortly after graduation from Greenwood High, she left home to attend Louisiana State Normal college. While there, during the last year of the existence of silent movies, she played the piano in a local movie theater for the silent ones.

"This was the Great Depression, and times were very harsh—millions of people were unemployed due to the terrible economy, and many died from starvation across the country. America was a Third World Country during the decade between 1929 and the early 1940s—when the War interrupted a nightmarish domestic scenario. The War did not save America's economy, that was accomplished by sound financial policies instituted by President Franklin D. Roosevelt, in conjunction with Speaker of the House Sam Rayburn and a few others in power during the War Years," Flournoy said.

"Mary was (like Lucien) unable to further her education for several years during the Great Depression. Later, she would attend summer school at LSU in Baton Rouge for several years, and worked as a teacher during the school year," according to the family documents.

Mary studied in Colorado and Texas universities, and for a time was an organist for the Rev. Billy Graham. She also had her own radio show—a 15-minute program titled: "Piano Impressions with Mary Flournoy."

During the War, she played piano for a while with a small band at Harmon General Hospital in Texas where there were several thousand wounded military personnel.

Alma Flournoy was born Aug. 14, 1914, in Greenwood. She was also christened at the Greenwood Methodist Church, but decided to become a Catholic later and was a member of the St. Francis Cabrini Catholic Church of Alexandria, Louisiana. She was smart, and started to school at age 5, finishing high school at age 15, and continued the family tendency of going into the teaching profession by attending Northwestern University in Natchitoches, Louisiana.

"The Great Depression of the Thirties was upon us, and this meant that barely enough money for clothes and tuition was available. We usually counted on the sale of bale cotton to pay for most of the fall entrance fees. Lillian was married by this time and Mary was teaching. Mary helped our mother with supporting the family," Alma wrote, for a family genealogist in the late 1970s.

"My high school principal persuaded me to change my plans from following the usual two-year elementary course to a four-year course—majoring in mathematics and chemistry. I did go on and get a degree in three years by working as a lab assistant and by going to school in the summers. After graduation, I—like my mother—was offered a scholarship, to the LSU graduate school, but could not consider it…," she wrote.

"Before I knew it, I was teaching in Greenwood at the ripe age of 19, and my students were my brother, Lucien, and his fourteen-year-old friends. We are now able to laugh about those days, but there were occasions when Lucien and I tried *to get home first* to tell our mother on the other!"

Alma would teach for almost five years in Greenwood, then was married in June 1938 to William James Rountree, of Gonzales, Louisiana.

Alma was a longtime member of the Girl Scouts, Cub Scouts, and many P.T.A. groups, and she was a member of the Louisiana Engineering Society. The youngest daughter, Laura, was born Feb. 21, 1917, in Greenwood, and was also christened at the Methodist Church—like everybody else. She was close in age to Lucien, so he learned a lot from her, too. Laura graduated from Greenwood High and Northwestern in Natchitoches, and worked several years as a stenographer for an oil company. But she also worked as a teacher—for 33 years—in Louisiana schools, mostly in Greenwood. The Flournoys were a very close family. According to the family records, Lucien was born in Greenwood, and graduated from high school there in May 1936. He was born in a Civil War-era antebellum house, and was a member of a family which had settled there technically in 1836, and carried one of the best-known names in Caddo Parish. Fortunately for the local area the huge Rodessa Oilfield was discovered during this period and after he graduated from high school, Flournoy went to work on drilling rigs in the area. The money he earned roughnecking during summers helped put him through three years at LSU ... before the Depression forced him out too, like his sister, Alma. They all knew real hardship, but also were intelligent and educated people, so they knew how to handle adversity pretty well. Like Flournoy's pioneer ancestors who settled Greenwood.

After he left LSU in 1939, Flournoy worked in Natchitoches, Baton Rouge, New Orleans, and a majority of the oil fields in the U.S., as a roughneck, truck driver, driller, tool-pusher and then advanced to well-logging engineer, drilling engineer, production engineer and finally reservoir engineer.

Just before his first trial run with the first rig he built, named "Old Bread and Butter", he and Maxine Edmonson were married.

"I asked Maxine to marry me (at that time) because I firmly believed my new rig would be successful right away, and it was," Flournoy said.

Between 1958 and 1977, Flournoy was contracted by Exxon and drilled 1,000 oil and gas wells in and around the million-acre King Ranch and that set the beat he would dance to during the banquet of life that he knew after the Exxon and King Ranch largesse rolled in to his Alice bank account.

In the late 1960s, he started Flournoy Production Company, and it initially operated 32 oil wells with average production at that time of 25,000 barrels per month, and 25 gas wells with average monthly production of 240,000 cubic feet of natural gas.

When we met in his office, he moved around in his chair restlessly, not always comfortable sitting and remembering. But he made this unusual experience an exception—knowing his time was short. He wanted to get his life story down before it was too late.

Pipeline Work

"As a boy, my mother took in boarders, and these were young men usually, from the nearby oilfields in Louisiana and across the Texas border. The roughnecks and oil rig workers always paid on time, or almost always, at the end of the month. But the pipeline workers would sometimes try to skip out at the end of the month without paying for their room and board and my mother needed that money badly. The farm needed it. One time a pipe-liner was in his car driving away without paying, and my mother climbed into our old car and chased him down the road and made him pay what he owed. I remember that one. She was a tough lady," he said. "But she had a big heart, as I mentioned."

Her full name before getting married was Lillie Ethel May, born April 27, 1879 in Cleveland, Arkansas. Her parents were Laura Briggs and Gabriel Andrew Jackson. She died March 11, 1965—age 86—after an illness. The world that Lucien Flournoy Sr., and Lillie May, were thrust into was harsh and hungry, with widespread diseases unchecked by early medicine. Lucien Sr. was the first of seven children, and his parents were Camp and Louise Wise Flournoy. He was born Feb. 23, 1872 in Caddo Parish—probably in the Greenwood area. He died Dec. 13, 1918, at home on the family farm just right outside Greenwood township. He and Lillie May were married Dec. 23, 1905 in Shreveport.

Their world was a stark contrast to the life into which their parents had been born. This new generation had no servants, and the Flournoy wealth had been largely dissipated by the late war (Civil War). This generation learned that, *by the sweat of thy brow shalt thou eat bread.* Long before his father, Civil War veteran Camp Flournoy, died in 1894, Lucien Sr., became strong and tough, and a good farm worker and rancher.

Lucien Sr.

Mary Flournoy said of her father, though she was only seven when he died, that she "never heard my father say a cross or unkind word to mother, and he would not argue, yet he was the boss. And my parents were people of high moral values."

Mary wrote that her mother, as a widow, was "a strong and courageous woman, reared (us) children, alone, and supported us by growing cotton on our farm and raising cows, chickens, and vegetables. She wanted her children to appreciate their heritage and she tried to instill in (us) the Christian values and the traits of their forefathers. Through great effort, sacrifice, and hardship she gave all five children a college education," she wrote.

Alma Flournoy wrote: "Lillie May came from Arkansas where she had taught in a one-room school house. She needed to go to teachers' college and was offered a scholarship but did not have the additional money required.

"She had a brother living in Shreveport so she moved there and found a job— sewing in a department store. There, Lillie met Lucien's sister, Gussie May, also a seamstress in the same store. The two became good friends and in time introduced each other to their future husbands. Gussie married Madison May, a cousin of Lillie's, and Lillie married Lucien," she wrote.

Lillie May

Lillie May was compassionate, but she was very savvy. She cared especially for the poor folks during the Depression when so many people were starving to death and out of work—about 10 million across the country, through no fault of their own—in most cases. Massive greed and terrible governmental policies—like modern day America—were mostly to blame for unemployment, homelessness, starvation, lack of any real medical care, especially in rural areas. She would always try to help people in tough times, hard situations.

Like his mother, Lucien and his sisters often longed for their father. He simply wanted to have an authoritative male presence there at the farm. But in learning about his father, he wanted to know him for who he was—a good man widely respected. His mother, though a beautiful young woman, never dated again or married. He was all the man she ever wanted, and she was that kind of a devoted and moral woman.

For many years Flournoy would take his private plane from Alice airport to the Shreveport Municipal airport, for trips back and forth between his two home towns.

In the early 2000s, Flournoy hired a plane to fly me and my wife Rowena, with his wife, to that place where he grew up. We landed at the Shreveport Municipal Airport on the first trip and were met by a farm foreman and we rode the half-hour through Shreveport on Interstate 20, to his farm house. His foreman, nicknamed "Red" was a soft-spoken man of about 70 years old or so, he had on a blue baseball cap, wore a big grin, had a casual shirt and blue jeans on, and wore running shoes. An amiable and highly loyal foreman for Flournoy--who was adept at finding the best kind of people. That single quality can make the difference between success in the harsh oil drilling business, and abject failure.

The old home place was well-kept with fresh paint, a new roof, and Flournoy had added an entire kitchen and bedrooms to the southern side adjacent to the main home, and that's where he and Maxine would stay, and where we all would dine together for breakfast and lunch. He'd take us all out to dinner, and Flournoy knew all the best places, too.

He had a very part-time housekeeper—we knew her only as Mary—and she lived somewhere nearby and was a polite and kindly young-looking woman the family had known for many years. Flournoy considered her "one of the family." Just like they did with Youree Hamilton, a black man just down the road, who'd lived there all his days. At that time, he was just about the same age as Flournoy.

And in return, the black people of that area *were not prejudiced* against the Flournoys, either. It was just friendship between families—regardless of color or race or religion, or anything else really. Most were plain old good people.

"You need to walk over and talk to Youree. He'll tell you stories, boy, about when we kids used to go skinny dipping—skinny boys swimming without underwear—in a local watering hole. It did not matter whether you were white or black, in that little pocket of time, and Youree and I have been friends most of our natural lives," Flournoy said.

On that first of several trips, we were joined by Flournoy's sister, Laura, who lived a few miles west of Greenwood in Waskom--a wide spot in the road.

He wanted us to meet several other family members, but most notably his last living sister, Laura, who grew up on the place.

Laura was helped by her youthfully middle-aged Triathlete son, Gene, into the detached kitchen and wood-paneled dining room near the main house. She sat down after seeing her brother again, exchanging pleasantries, and Lucien kept standing to introduce her to me, my wife, and a few other lunch guests that summer afternoon of long ago.

The expansive, self-dramatic, elder sister wanted to make her presence clear. She was strong-willed, too. Her high pitched, unpleasant elderly voice, started calmly, then she became more forceful--almost shouting around the large wooden table, spitting the words out so that I guarded my sandwich with an open hand: "When LUCIEN was born, Lord it was the son—the S-U-N—and brought my mother out of the darkness. He was the sunshine. We finally had a man in the house, who would help us girls milk the cows and the..."

Lucien sat silently, not looking at Laura, but he heard what she said. He'd been leaning back in the chair, but shifted his weight forward and the chair's legs hit the wooden floor. You could hear it pretty well. It punctuated Laura's sentence.

"EXCUSE ME...excuse me...," he said, his voice betraying a slight irritation.

But his sister just kept on, as if she didn't hear him. They'd always been like that, from childhood, I later learned from other relatives and friends.

"Yes, the dark clouds of death parted and the SUN shined for all of us in the..."

He was the baby brother and she always regarded him as such, no matter how successful he was, but Flournoy spoke out a little more aggressively.

"Excuse me, Laura dear," he touched her right shoulder. She was sitting close to him. He turned toward her, then back to the guests—about six or eight of us—munching on cold cuts, and potato chips, washed down liberally with large glasses of iced tea.

She was solicitous of her baby brother all her life, but they also evidently liked to argue, and while we were all trying to eat that afternoon after arriving from Shreveport, she started telling us how she and her sisters would help out on the farm. This elicited a rather negative response from Flournoy as he lowered the sandwich, hovering uneasily near the plate below him as he hunched forward a little.

"He was the son, you know. When he was born it was like the sun rising," she said, in a kind of sarcastic tone. He caught on to that right quick.

"Laura, now you know I did all the hard work around the farm. You girls helped around the house, but I did most of the work," Flournoy said.

Laura just kept on as if he hadn't said anything: "Yes, he was the sun shining, when he was born...."

Flournoy glared straight ahead and tried to keep focused on his hunger and the damned ham sandwich, his emotional fuse lit already, and finally turned to Laura and they started arguing about who did what, around the farm. The pleasant façade faded. He was in his early 80s and she was almost two years older. No one dared interfere with this brother and sister *happening*. I almost laughed out loud at one point, but managed to lower my head and stifle everything but a slight smile. The two siblings were oblivious to us anyway.

"Laura, you know I was the only one who ever worked on this place. You and Lillian, Mary and Alma, you girls did a lot of work but when I was old enough, mother put me in charge of the farm work," he said, looking around at us, one by one, and lowering his head to stare at each of us listeners for a moment. He wanted to make sure we understood. We nodded.

Laura sat listening to him but didn't let it stop her. She was on a roll.

"You helped us girls, you sure did, and mother. Well, we just couldn't have made it," she said.

Again, he spoke up, his volume a little louder. He looked up at the ceiling and finally deferred to his big sister, to some degree. But the sibling rivalry was alive and well in these octogenarians.

"Sister, after I was old enough, I did ALL the work around here outside," he said as Mary, the old family friend, crept around from person to person silently, filling up empty tea glasses.

He looked straight at me and winked. I knew it was just their thing. They always did that; Maxine would tell me later: "He does get overbearing."

Finally, Flournoy pushed his chair back from the large oak table and excused himself to take a bathroom break. That ended the exchange, but my wife and I were kicking each other under the table to try and keep from laughing out loud. It was humorous being witness to the two squabbling over ancient memories, old times, but beneath that was their deep affection and love for one another and that's what we all knew—Maxine knew it. The prospect of either of them dying was a menacing thought to both, as it is to most siblings, and parents, and the rip tides of time were preparing to take them down, and they knew it well.

All the while, outside the main house, an oil jack kept pace with the conversations, as if it pumped many barrels of oil every day. It was a well that Flournoy drilled years before for his mother. The shadows of that tall pump jack as it seesawed the black liquid from down below could be seen through the drapes of that kitchen while we dined. He said it wasn't much of a well, and maybe he just drilled it as a symbol of what he'd done with his life. Something his mother would love—and she did, too.

We could hear the commode flushing in a nearby bathroom and Flournoy returned to the table. He moved slowly, but made his way to the chair across from us, with his back to those drapes and the shadows of that pump jack as it quietly worked while we ate our food and listened and talked.

When the odor from Flournoy's bathroom-break reached us at the table, Laura was the first one to speak up.

"What HAVE you been eating, brother? Lord. Did you shut the door?" I almost choked on my sandwich. Flournoy changed the subject.

"When my father died in December 1918, during that terrible epidemic, the girls were not allowed to attend his burial at the family cemetery about a mile away. The danger was too great that they'd get the flu virus, too, so my mother asked the funeral director to have the horse-drawn hearse with my father's coffin, to pass by our house so the girls and my pregnant mother could look out the windows and say goodbye. The girls had to stand on their tip-toes as my dad's body passed by, the horses blowing steam from the cold and the work of hauling that heavy hearse," Flournoy said, commandeering the conversation—as he often did. As the little brother, he was sometimes afforded that luxury around the house even from a young age. Not seriously spoiled, but it was his personality to take charge. Something probably learned from watching and taking orders from his strong and spirited mother.

After a couple of hours, Flournoy and his sister said their goodbyes as Gene helped to the driveway and their car. They each hugged and she waved as her son drove them away. Flournoy watched as the car backed out, and reached the end of the long driveway, and waved again as it moved along the road out of sight.

"Nothing of a man but pyramids, can afford to laugh at time" —Mark Twain

CHAPTER 5

We returned to the new guest addition of the house, built a few years before, and sat at our chairs in the coolness of the air-conditioned room. The hum of the window units as they cooled the air almost lulled us to sleep as we sat for a while, and suddenly—a knock at the door. No one heard DeOrsay Simpson's car when he arrived in it, but my wife opened the kitchen door and there he was—Flournoy's oldest best boyhood friend. A tall and thin man, with a full head of gray hair, rather long, and bushy eyebrows, and big white teeth and a smile that put them on full display as he spoke and laughed remembering old times with Flournoy.

He and Flournoy shook hands, and he hugged Maxine, and met everybody, then sat at a chair on the right side of Flournoy. They talked together a few minutes and then started remembering. DeOrsay wanted this in the book.

"Let me tell you what we used to do. Well, you see, we had this old Model T Ford that we'd welded together—it was two cars cut in half and we welded the two good ends together, but it would run and we didn't even have a license, but we'd drive those old country roads, dirt roads, all the time as teenagers. We had a problem with gas money, so we'd carry a gas can with us, a siphoning hose, and a sign we made that said, "Out of Gas" in the car. And then when we'd finally run out, we'd put out that sign, and in those days people would always stop. So, they'd ask if we needed a ride and we'd say we just need a gallon or so of gas. And if they said it was OK, we'd whip out the hose and can and lickety split we'd have a gallon or so of gas and we'd thank the people and we'd be on our way again," DeOrsay said, bumping Flournoy with his elbow as they sat at the table together.

Flournoy smiled and raised his eyebrows as he looked at me again.

As if to say, "Boy, you didn't know we were wild young men, did you?" I knew. Having been one myself, and a country boy to boot. Flournoy and I were the same in many ways, and that's why he hired me to write his biography. He knew from the minute we met for the interview in his office, after I drove the long distance from Albuquerque to Alice—just to shake hands and talk.

"Remember when we jacked up the back of the postmaster's mail truck, so the wheels were about an inch off the driveway, when he was in the post office, and sat back in the bushes to wait for him to load the mail truck up and get in and he put the truck in reverse and it wouldn't move? He could not figure it out! He kept walking around and around that truck wondering what the hell was wrong. We were back there laughing so hard, he almost heard us," Flournoy said.

DeOrsay burst out with a big laugh, and the incandescent smile, like a light that brightened up the gloom of history and old age. Both men laughed as Maxine smiled across from Flournoy, with a look that seemed to say this was all new to her. And it may have been. Or perhaps a note of sarcasm, too.

God only knows how many pranks those two men pulled around town when they were young boys and teenagers.

"Our high school mascot was the "Tadpoles" but we were already full-grown bullfrogs by the time we graduated," DeOrsay said. "And we liked to jump just about any young female that would have us."

The only time, Flournoy said, that he got into trouble was when the high school was staging a big band concert in the auditorium one night when he was a student at the Greenwood High. It's a little hard to believe he only got into trouble that one time. Sometimes he had a convenient memory, though he never lied about anything important—family, or business dealings. He did sometimes stretch the truth a little, as Maxine would readily attest after she rolled her eyes at some of his stories.

DeOrsay verified this one.

"There was a kid who played the tuba, and he was getting ready to go on stage in front of the packed crowd of parents and teachers and assorted kids, and for some reason Lucien didn't care for the boy and so while the kid went to the rest room, and left the tuba sitting there, Lucien got the crazy idea to stuff the tuba with a bunch of paper. He was laughing while he was doing it. I told him he was gonna to get a whomping from his mother but he just said *shut up* and *let's get the hell out of here.* We went out into the crowd so we could hear, and when that kid's time came, he went out there proudly, with his big tuba, this tall, skinny kid, with pimples on his proud face, and he tried to blow into that tuba but no sound came out. He tried several times, and finally a teacher walked out and fetched him and back stage they discovered what had happened. We were stifling our laughter. It was outrageous. Some people were chuckling and laughing in the crowd, a little, and we decided it was time for us to make a graceful exit. We tried, but everybody knew. They could tell this was the work of the pranksters. We got into some big trouble over that one," DeOrsay said.

Maxine, sitting a few feet away from me, laughed at that one. She could definitely believe it, and you could tell from the look on her face. The laughter faded into a smile and she shook her head slightly as she looked over at DeOrsay.

"I would believe it. Knowing him, I would believe that one," she said to him, as he sat next to Flournoy, again hitting him on his shoulder—not hard, but enough to convey his revival of youthful exuberance.

Finally, after an hour of visiting, Flournoy stood up from the dinner table chair in the cool room. He suggested we take a little ride around town and see what was going on. DeOrsay agreed it was a good idea, as he usually did when his old buddy suggested something. He always looked up to his boyhood friend, even into old age. Flournoy was a natural leader, and that was clear to anyone. Not overly bossy, never a bully, he led with competence and courage, without having to say much.

He was the level-headed Andy Griffith, like the de facto sheriff of the small-town Greenwood, the man everybody could depend on to be there when it counted, with his competent, laid-back leadership—a natural ability. DeOrsay was a little more like Barney Fife, somewhat excitable, but always at Flournoy's side to do his bidding, if need be, and always loyal. Always.

Though he didn't have much as a boy, Lucien did have a bicycle, he said, as we all loaded into his 1980s style Chevy Suburban, parked on the concrete driveway in behind the house. He backed out, still talking, with everyone listening. He turned the air-conditioner on high, to force out the hot, humid Louisiana air. He clicked the truck in drive and hit the gas, jerking our heads back. He drove like a madman.

"One day, my dare-devil side caught up with me. In full view of a lady named Jane McClurg. She was the grandmother of Bill Peters," he said, touching DeOrsay on the left shoulder as he turned to him at a stop sign.

"DeOrsay, you remember Bill." Both men nodded.

"That old lady was full-blooded Irish, and she talked like it, too," Flournoy said, laughing, as he whizzed through a few streets in the small town, on that lazy hot afternoon. Lucien saw two people sitting on a front porch, in the shade, and recognized them immediately—though he hadn't seen them in years.

"That's Bill there," he said, stopping the truck. He didn't need to unbuckle the dangling seat belt, rolled the window down and yelled, as he slammed the automatic shifter in park, cut the engine and climbed out. We followed him out, into the front lawn.

"This is Bill, and Eva, his wife. Bill Peters. We've known each other for ages," Lucien said. DeOrsay smiled and shook hands with Bill, followed by Lucien.

"We grew up with him," DeOrsay said, as my wife and I exchanged smiles with the kindly old couple.

"Lou, dontcha think ah, you found a good parking space?" Bill Peters said as he pointed to the brown and tan Suburban, parked in the middle of the street.

Lucien hadn't bothered to pull over to the side. He didn't care about breaking small rules if it served some larger purpose. A trait from boyhood that probably served him well in life.

He smiled and noted that Greenwood's police department was small and "this is the weekend anyway. It's Sunday, and God bless Saint Peter."

We all gathered around on the front porch and Lucien and Bill talked a while, then Lucien remembered the story he was about to tell us. As he brought it up, Eva Peters had the details—as if even people's thoughts in that small community were connected some kind of way. A lot more human than the internet, Facebook, or anything electronic.

"Yes, Lucien was going down to John May's Cotton Gin. There were two gins in those days, down by the railroad tracks. The road was gravel, and car tires will make tracks and build up gravel high in the center. So,

Lucien was probably being cute, showing out. He hit some loose gravel in any case and when he did that the bicycle went sideways down, and down he went," she said. "He just wrecked and skinned his knees. She (Mrs. McClurg) didn't ask him if he was scraped or hurt, just kept walking past. All she said, in her thick Irish accent was: 'An dawn waint anotter boy.'"

This made us all laugh, and Lucien remembered it well.

"She said that, and then she just turned and walked away to wherever it was she was headed. I picked up the bike, dusted myself off, and limped back home," he said.

Flournoy – Wise House

Greenwood, Caddo Parish, LA
Donna Fricker
April 1989
LA SHPO

Photo # 1

South-Southwest

Flournoy – Wise House

Greenwood, Caddo Parish, LA
Donna Fricker
April 1989
LA SHPO

Photo #2

Northwest

Flournoy – Wise House

Greenwood, Caddo Parish, LA
Donna Fricker
April 1989
LA SHPO

Photo # 3

Interior View – Central Hall

Flournoy – Wise House

Greenwood, Caddo Parish, LA
Donna Fricker
April 1989
LA SHPO

Photo # 4

Interior View – Mantel

After about an hour, it was time to head back to the Flournoy house, only a few blocks away. My wife and I went to our room in the old big house, and DeOrsay and Lucien went into the detached kitchen area, where they remained for hours. The visiting for us was done for that day. And it had been a long and enjoyable time. I read through a few notebooks, where I'd written what he'd said in our interviews, and found an old newspaper article in that bedroom about one of Flournoy's local stalwart relatives named J. Howell Flournoy. Later, I'd ask Flournoy about him.

Caddo Parish Sheriff J. Howell Flournoy, the longest serving sheriff in parish history to the present time, was born October 21, 1890 at

Greenwood. He was the son of James Patteson Flournoy (born August 25, 1853 in Tennessee) and his wife, Georgia Elizabeth Martin (born November 1, 1852) of Caddo Parish.

Like most of the Louisiana Flournoys, J. Howell attended elementary school in Greenwood. He first worked as a mechanic at Wray Ford Company in Shreveport. His father, an early automobile owner, obtained the job for his son so J. Howell would learn how to maintain his own car later on and *he paid the boy's salary after the dealership found out he was not a trained mechanic.*

"He then worked with Gulf Refining Company as a time keeper, riding horseback 40 to 50 miles daily along the Satello and Fort Worth pipe line," according to Caddo Parish records. "In 1913 he joined the Caddo Sheriff's Department as a deputy, serving until 1916 when his Army National Guard unit, Company L, was called into service along the Mexican Border. After the U.S. became involved in the Great War (later known as World War I) in 1917 against Germany, J. Howell joined up and was a machine gun instructor at Camp Hancock, Georgia, where the Army commissioned him a lieutenant.

After returning from Army service, J. Howell went back to work for the Caddo Parish Sheriff's Department, and in 1940 was elected sheriff—a position he held until his December 1966 death from illness in Caddo Parish.

"Long concerned with young people, Sheriff Flournoy some years ago prepared and published a booklet entitled, 'Winning Our Youth'". The booklet was widely published, and in 1960 was read into the Congressional Record," according to Caddo Parish official records.

"Sheriff J. Howell was my cousin, but he never did me any personal favors and I wouldn't have asked him to," Flournoy said, looking at me from across his desk—his mind peering into the long ago past as he seemed to resent my presence in his dining room. "He couldn't have helped me against my mother, if I did something bad, regardless."

Sheriff Flournoy was a deputy in Caddo Parish when the famous black singer Leadbelly—Huddie Ledbetter—was sometimes finding leisure and comfort in the party area for black people in Shreveport. He even liked Leadbelly's songs—especially the one he wrote for Texas Governor Allred specifically with the idea that Allred would like the song and reconsider Leadbelly's long prison stretch—he was convicted of killing a black man one night with a small caliber revolver. Gov. Allred loved the song, and signed an order pardoning Leadbelly when the Governor got back to Austin. This true story was in the TV movie and a biography about Leadbelly from some years ago.

Deputy Flournoy was sometimes called to take care of problems in the black area of Shreveport—that party place—but Leadbelly was always friendly to him, he told fellow lawmen who scoffed at the thought of a white man being surprised that a black man was less than obsequious. Leadbelly held his head up high, and he stood tall even among white people of the day. To him—tough as hell—he was as good as anybody. Deputy Flournoy agreed.

Flournoy spoke about J. Howell for quite a while, then he picked up the telephone near the table, a landline of course, and started talking oil business—without warning. I took that as my cue to slip on out of range—down range of his booming battleship cannon voice. Around six feet tall, he had the body of a heavy-set, strong man, but the voice of a giant. Many a time I'd be nodding off at my office desk after lunch—mid-afternoon—and would he shocked awake like pissing on an electric fence as he would shout: "FLORES!" And I'd grab my pen and notebook and lurch back into the fray.

During and after World War II, Sheriff Flournoy sometimes had his department busy handling the many veterans from North Louisiana who were either leaving for war, or coming home from war—either the European or Pacific Theaters of Operation.

"When (my brother) came back from Europe after fighting all through the Battle of the Bulge with the 101st Airborne, he was like a lot of fellow paratroopers and blew off a lot of steam on the weekends, especially. I remember sometimes the law would look the other way, and let (the soldiers and Marines) have their fun—up to a point," said my father, Carl Flores, in a 2017 interview at his ranch house in Johnson County, Texas—near the small town of Grandview.

My father's brother was Louis B. Flores, born in the small rural community of Rambin, located about 30 miles south of Shreveport, in the deep woods of DeSoto Parish. His nickname was Shorty, a name he took from a local character named Red Shorty, as a young boy. He had a mind of his own, as my father would say with a laugh.

"Those boys would sometimes raise hell, and I was just barely old enough to drive, so I'd have to go get him out of trouble, but he never got into trouble with Sheriff Flournoy. Shorty and his friends, many were veterans and cousins, would go to Shreveport or just stay in Mansfield where they knew the law would look the other way, and they did a lot of times," he said.

Sheriff Flournoy was also fair-minded when it came to race and class. To him, people were all about the same, regardless of their bank accounts, or their color or class status.

"J. Howell stopped a white mob from lynching a black man on the Caddo Parish Courthouse grounds," Flournoy said.

"This was during a time of terrible racism throughout the south, when the KKK and other white supremacists would use lynching as a tool to keep the black people oppressed— or in their view, to 'keep the negroes in line'. This was nothing short of terrorism on the part of the KKK," he said.

"We were from educated people, smart people who knew that the best way to get along with people was to treat others the way you want them to treat you … the Golden Rule. After the Civil War, southerners lost their way of life, along with a lot of land, and without slaves to look down on, the white man began to hate the black man, and started to resent blacks in general. As the white population suffered, their seething hatred resulted in mobs of whites hunting for black people—especially males—and either beating them up or killing them through shooting, lynching, burning, or all three," Flournoy said.

"Pure and plain ignorance, and stupidity. That's the basis of racism, where it's born and bred," Flournoy said. "We learned that from my mother, as children. My father believed that way, too."

After Sheriff Flournoy died, Bossier City Police Chief James Cathey said: "We have lost one of the most dedicated of law enforcement officers anywhere in the United States.

CHAPTER 6

SOLID LOUISIANA BOY

In the old main house bed-room we slept in, I later found a book in a shelf by the large four-poster bed, titled: "How to Like People" by World War II veteran Robert Jackson, printed in 1962 by Crowell-Collier Press. I read the book twice, and realized why it was in the Flournoy family book shelf. This was something that Lucien Flournoy had read, and re-read, and memorized. He knew it was vital for his personal and professional life to find ways to like even the most dislikeable people—and there were plenty of those types in the oilfields and in politics. He combined such techniques with his natural positive personality and it helped him a lot over the years.

Jackson dedicated the book: "…for us who need to join humanity and find more freedom." After reading the book, I think Flournoy could have written it just by what he knew on his own about people, and life, and though he could sometimes be bossy and egocentric, his ego in crucial matters, to him, meant nothing. Far more important was the larger world outside his own small self. His I.Q. was 128, so he had plenty of brain power to figure the world out pretty well—to understand and want to get along with people.

When I later presented the book to Flournoy, he smiled and held court at the dinner table as he quoted: "'Most of us think we have a Great Love for our Fellow Man, but we don't *like* people, don't really enjoy them, don't *talk* to them, don't *see* them. We don't have any idea how much they mean to us. Yet we have to be a part of humanity to be truly alive,'" Flournoy quoted him. "'Well, all right, we know all that. But we forget it, expect to live it some other day. We have people all around us, chances for simple friendliness, for life itself, but with all this money in the bank we think we're broke.'"

This was before Coronavirus in spring 2020 reared its devilish head in America—and the world—just as the flu had done in winter 1918 taking Flournoy's good strong 47-year-old father down, fast and hard. The euphemism "social distancing" became the name of the game. Flournoy would have said simply: *do not touch anybody with a ten-foot pole.*

"'… belonging to humanity is not just good for you. It's a big favor to everyone you meet, Jackson wrote,'" Flournoy said.

Too bad most of our national "leaders", evidently, have never read this book. Or if they have, somehow, they've totally missed the entire point. Possibly willfully. That's how world wars get started. Another aspect of Flournoy's character was simply this good will toward others.

"'Good will is *not* trying-to-please. It is not being nice and sweet and adaptable. What it *is* is wishing the best for everyone, and *no exceptions.* Any words or actions that don't come from good will come from some other will—the will to force someone into a mold, the urge to strike back, the desire to run and hide, the aim to deceive, or the like. You always have a will. What is it right now?'" Jackson wrote—according to Flournoy.

Flournoy said: "I almost memorized that entire book, and I'm a slow reader. So that took a while."

Though he was a wealthy man, Flournoy never lost a certain humility and politeness, courtesy, that he learned growing up, and it was also just who he was—he never changed his basic personality and was fully aware of the forces that often do change people, like too much money, power, fame, success. Often, he'd seen all that go to people's heads—and it invariably ruined them. He never let that happen, and probably tried hard to make sure it didn't. Many of his drilling competitors in the Alice area were often underbid by Flournoy, because he was not greedy, either. Flournoy—except for a few people he admitted that he hated with a passion, and for good reason—had true good will for most everybody he met, or knew, or employed, or served in public office as Alice mayor.

Flournoy finally sold his drilling company, after 50 years in business, on January 31, 1997 to a Houston oil company named Greywolf. At that time, Flournoy Drilling was the oldest independent oil company in the state and the nation under one owner the entire time, and it was a huge boost to the Alice economy for years—the largest employer along with the school district.

Though he usually tried to like most people—not all, but most—when he took my wife and I out to a catfish restaurant near Greenwood one night, just us three, he blurted out: "nothing is more repulsive than the sound of people eating. Nothing quite as squalid sounding. Like the same sound of somebody on the commode with a bad case of diarrhea ... YUKKKK," he said out loud, in his booming voice. He seemed not to care who heard him. I almost choked on my catfish. It really was hard to eat around him, because he made the most outrageously humorous observations so much of the time. He was bluntly hilarious so much of the time—seeming to not even be aware of it. Or he had the style to not dress up his humor with his own laughter.

Flournoy's Corpus Christi oilfield buddy, W. Carlton Weaver (he liked the nickname "Tubby" from his college days), knew Flournoy well. They were close friends and associates, and helped each other out a lot of times. Tubby was a tall and fit man, about six feet, with a Hill Country drawl and an easy personality, and he was a top intellect, as well as a geologist and into many other areas. He knew how to effectively work with landowners for rights.

A few weeks after we returned from Greenwood, my wife and I were invited by Tubby to come visit him at his condo near the old downtown Corpus Christi overlooking Corpus Christi Bay. From there, he drove us in his Cadillac a short distance to the Bayfront Yacht Club, where we had a fine dinner. He was a philosopher, on top of everything else, but I would say he liked to make observations about anything in life. You couldn't any more stop Tubby from talking, then you could have stopped the Titanic from sinking. The same went for Flournoy and DeOrsay—but the laughter made it worth the while.

"The world outside wants to convince us that anything inside is false, that only material is real. The society we live in fears nothing more collectively than a true individual who lives with conviction and courage. That's the toughest road to take, but the only way to the truth. Knowing what not to do is just as important as knowing what to do," he said to us, as he chewed his fish. Tubby, the catfish-crunching philosopher. Aristotle, with anchovies on the side. And a few vodka martinis to lubricate the semi-mechanical subject of conversation.

"Flournoy has this simplicity of deportment, and a glowing sincerity. It's deeply moving," he said, with a tone of sarcasm in his voice.

Tubby, though slowed by time and decades of hard work in the oilfields, walked with the confidence of a brave captain in the fortress just before a dawn attack. His voice cut urgent and clean, always up-to-speed, always accessible.

"Let me tell you young people something I've learned along the way ... the mysteries of the human heart are like shadows in a moonlit forest. Life is inscrutable, enigmatic, relentless, and you'd better be on your game. Flournoy is always on his," Tubby said. "And there are no degrees of honorable. You either are, or you aren't. The greatest thing a man can ever own is a good reputation."

In observing Tubby, it occurred to me in a flash that if the feeling is there, full expression will flower. He was a real storyteller—like Flournoy—painting in bold and haunting and exciting colors.

"Flournoy is charming, but sometimes vicious. To some, he is impossible. He has uncompromising standards, and is an idealist about life and especially about his dreams, but a pragmatist when it comes to day-to-day engineering of his business," he added, chomping on some kind of odd-looking side dish.

My mind returned to that Louisiana catfish joint and what Flournoy said so vociferously about the sound of people eating.

"Flournoy has all the innocence of a Molotov cocktail," Tubby said, looking up from his dish at my wife, then at me, as his smile widened and he stuffed his face a little more—but with the manners of royalty. He could have dined with Queen Elizabeth just the same as a homeless bum sharing a Poor Boy sandwich. Titles and status meant little to him. The oil business meant everything—it was his passion.

Tubby had a wide smile, big teeth, wore glasses, and dressed in a fine suit and tie on the evening that we dined at the Yacht Club. He had a power and rhythm of language that held his listeners spellbound—an eccentric and intellectual wit of rare talent and expression.

Tubby had a job—oilfield geologist and speculator—that was his brand of authoritative masculinity, and he carried the crown of great success jauntily. He was a good listener, too. Singer-songwriter Kris Kristofferson once said of Willie Nelson: "He wears the world like a loose garment." That was Tubby.

He'd been married 40 or 50 years to a good woman, but she'd died some years before. We met-up with him again when he stopped by Flournoy's office one afternoon a few weeks after our dinner. He was old enough by that time to just speak whatever was on his mind at any given moment: "Don't ever cheat on your wife, because she will always find out and it just makes a mess out of everything, for everybody. That kind of selfishness can be deadly in more ways than you can imagine—your health, your wealth, your joy, love, trust, everything goes away," he said. "If you love somebody enough to marry them, and have kids, then be true to yourself. That way, you will be true to your wife."

Flournoy was not in the office that day, but Tubby was driving across South Texas on oil and gas business and decided to stop by the office. He was sent to the conference room in the back of the building behind Flournoy's office, where my desk and computer were located. We talked a while.

"Lou used to drink a lot. I did too, but I wasn't into it like he was. He finally had to cut it out, and one day, fairly recently, I was driving by the Flournoy's house and he was just pulling in. We got to talking and I asked if he was still off the bottle—I hadn't met up with him in a while. We were just joking around. He said he was still dry as a bone. So, I asked him about his other problem—women—and asked if he'd given up chasing them. He grinned and said, 'Well, I can't give up everything.'"

Tubby, at that time he was 90, had a girlfriend in Houston and he drove everywhere—all over South Texas and including visits to San Antonio, and Houston.

"One day I was late getting to Houston to see my woman friend, driving my Cadillac about 90 miles per hour along Interstate 10, and I looked in the rear view mirror and it was a motorcycle cop with his lights on for me to pull over," Tubby said, chuckling as he sat back from his dinner. "I had a dozen roses beside me for my gal friend and when the cop walked up to my window, he said I was speeding and wanted my driving license. I gave it to him, and he smiled and handed it back and told me at my age I ought to watch out for that high speed. He asked me where I was going in such a hurry. I pointed to the dozen red roses beside me and said, 'I've got a date with my lady friend and I am very late.' The officer smiled even more, and saluted me, and said to slow her down a bit and he wishes me good luck, but no speeding ticket. I got lucky. That was a lucky day."

In the year that my wife and I spent with Flournoy and his colorful and highly interesting friends and colleagues, I would get to know Tubby well, and he reminded me of my grandfather—who was a roughneck in the 1920s, working in Louisiana for Standard Oil Company. He died Dec. 1992 at age 92.

"Let me tell you, sometimes it could get pretty rough out there drilling. I was running a rig in San Patricio County—South Texas—and we had a cable tool rig set up and were making some hole but were running low on food for the crews. I was head of the operation, as the tool-pusher or rig manager—whatever you want to call it in modern terms. So, it fell on me to go into the nearest town and buy some food and hopefully find some strong men to replace a few who had walked out on me. When their bellies started to growl, those guys started to howl. I told them to hit the road," Tubby said.

"I was driving the flatbed truck around the town, the county seat, and circled it and went right past a tall, big, man with a nice dark suit and tie, a cowboy hat, smoking a big cigar, and he gave me a look that I didn't particularly care for, so I went around the square again, and he glared at me again. I stopped and this important-looking man asked what I was looking for, and I told him it was none of his goddamned business. So, he took off his coat and hat and glasses, sat them in a small pile beside him, and that was my cue to exit the truck," he said, his smile widening as he lowered his gray old full head of hair and lifted it back up chuckling.

"Well, then, here's my flask. Have a drink with me," the man said. "I turned around and said, 'I have to go.'" Well, that pissed him off. That did it.

"I was a strong young buck, and not afraid of anybody, and we went after it for a few minutes. He'd hit me and I'd hit him, and we'd roll around a little, and finally we wouldn't get back up, but a Mexican boy came and helped us up. Me and then him. He turned out to be the county judge. He dusted himself off, we were both breathing hard, and asked me what I was in town for, and I said I needed some food and some workers, but just at that time it started to flood. Raining cats and dogs and rabbits and every wild thing, and the judge just let out a loud whistle. All of a sudden, out of nowhere, but from everywhere, about six or eight young Mexican guys just appeared from various places nearby. He told the men I'd hire 'em if they were ready to work. Back then good pay was hard to find but any steady money was a lot better than riding a horse for a living—getting paid very little, sporadically, doing brutal work for 14 hours a day. And those poor Mexican boys worked hard and couldn't speak English. They might make a dollar a day," Weaver said. He could pay them more than that—plus all the food they could eat.

"The judge handed me a key and pointed to the San Patricio County Courthouse, and said, "this opens the door to the jury dormitory, where we have to keep the juries sequestered—locked away from the public to prevent jury influencing, tampering. He said I could sleep in one of the beds there if it kept raining. Back then roads were terrible all-over South Texas and the Valley. The rain flooded the river between me and my men and the rig, so I turned around and drove back and slept that night in the jury dorm of the courthouse. Later the next day, I was able to cross the river, and brought new men and beans and bacon, and corn and dove, and rabbits, whatever I could procure from farmers growing corn in big fields—without their knowledge many times. But it was essential that we had some food. I would shoot dove in those same big fields and my men ate well most of the time. I got to be very good at scrounging things. That was a tough go, that well in San Patricio."

This biography could be subtitled: *Maxine and Tubby* because their stories are highly colorful and relevant to the Flournoy life of adventure and hard work, and a lot of good times.

"It was October 1945 and Tenneco completed the first long distance pipeline from Aqua Dulce, Texas, to West Virginia—or 1,265 miles," Tubby said. "It was a seminal event for South Texas. First natural gas ever every pipelined long distance. That right there was a big help to developing our country. And the wars later provided the tremendous sudden demand for oil and gas. You know there are two factors in business—PUT and TAKE. If you take something out, put something back. I think it's important," Weaver said.

"And I remember the atmosphere of those early days in Corpus Christi, the geologists, engineers, pipeline welders, all kinds of technology showing up. I remember a man was allowed, in the oilfield work, to only work six hours a day, but he got a minimum wage of $5 a day. Dang good money in those times when the world was black and blue from a Great Depression and Hitler's Disease. And the Japs wanted us too. It was a lot more critical than things are today, even with this Bush economy. Americans were tough then, farm people, simple, good people for the most part. People tended to be friends and enjoy life, it seemed to me. That's sad. But Texas oil helped greatly to win that terrible war, it really did. British Prime Minister Winston Churchill said: "` (The American Allies) have floated us to victory on an ocean of oil.'"

Tubby admitted he had to be tight-fisted with his money in those tough times, when he was starting out in the oil business as a young rig manager: I paid 'em $5 a day but worked 'em 12 hours anyhow. I was feeding them good and that kept the men around the rig. Food was tough to come by in those times. I shot more dove, for our food, I didn't eat another dove for 20 years."

Tubby almost got into trouble with the law over working his men 12 hours, he said, and just about the time he was going to trial over the problem, the U.S. Supreme Court ruled it not unconstitutional as long as he paid wages he owed: "The Supreme Court ruled on that case only a few days before my trial. OK? That was kinda close."

CHAPTER 7

LONG YEARS OF WINE AND ROSES

He could often be bossy, and stubborn, and sometimes had a bad temper, but after chewing one of his employees out, later Flournoy would go back and apologize— whether he was wrong or not. And sometimes he'd give that person a big bonus in their next paycheck.

A former Alice resident named A. Salas wrote the following in 2009 about an encounter he had with Flournoy at the apex of the oilman's power and wealth, while working at an Alice grocery store as a clerk/manager. This tells a lot about Flournoy:

"It is embarrassing to admit that I was twenty-seven years old before I learned who Lucien Flournoy, the man, was. Back then the Flournoy name was familiar -- famous really. It still is. His company had a payroll that was spread far and wide, but that was about all I knew. Anyone in this area was familiar with his name, his company and his philanthropy, but my head wasn't screwed on too well in the summer of 1980 and all that familiarity escaped me. When I look back on my condition thirty or so years ago, I can only shake my head. That was a rough year. The realization of how ignorant a young man I was pains me. It is one reason I cut many of these young fellows a lot of slack these days," Salas wrote.

"In the spring of 1980 I was working three jobs in order to meet my obligations. You can do that when you're young, and still have the energy to go dancing on Saturday night. At the end of that school year I resigned from my teaching job with the Alice ISD in Alice, Texas. There would be no bus route to drive in the morning or in the afternoon when the new school year came around. That was my second job. I'd had enough of that. I committed myself to full-time employment with HEB Grocery Company. That had been my third job after the bus route. Now I could give the company 110%. I was one, of two, night-managers at the old Alice store at First and Almond. HEB was a tough and demanding outfit to work for back then, but the benefits were great. At the time I thought it was a good call.

"The store had a check-cashing policy that limited our customers to cashing a personal check for amounts no greater than $25. The ceiling for payroll checks was $350; local entities only. The office employees, me included, adhered to the policy religiously -- no exceptions. It was the rule. There was no need to call Jesse Salazar, the store manager, to approve exceptions. It just wasn't done. If a customer proved troublesome, we simply fell back on the policy. Sorry, rules are rules," he wrote.

"One afternoon a well-dressed gentleman in a fine suit, flanked by what I took to be two subordinates, both equally dressed, stepped up to the office counter. One look told me this wasn't the everyday HEB customer. As usual, we were extremely busy on the checkout floor and in the office.

"Yes, sir. How can I help you?", I asked.

"Yes. Thank you. Would you permit me to cash a personal check?"

"Yes, sir, of course," I replied.

"The gentleman slipped a checkbook from inside his jacket, flipped it open on the counter with one hand and pulled a pen out his breast pocket with the other. They each seemed to match in design, the checkbook and the pen. I don't know why that image has stayed with me all these years.

"Will five-hundred be acceptable?"

"He hadn't begun to write on the blank check. I paused for only a second before stating the store policy to the man," Salas wrote. "Our limit is twenty-five dollars on personal checks, sir."

Flournoy's face registered no emotion.

"I assure you the check is good for the amount." Flournoy's tone was calm, measured.

"I'm sorry, sir. That's the store policy -- only twenty-five dollars on personal checks."

"Oh, I see." He paused for a second. "I take it you cash payroll checks here?" Salas wrote that he had a bad feeling about this. The line of customers requiring office service was growing behind this man, and it seemed as though every eye was on him.

"You cash payroll checks for Flournoy Drilling, I take it?" He continued.

"Yes, sir. We do," Salas said he told Flournoy—very cool about it all.

"How interesting. Up to what amount?"

"We cash payroll checks for up to $350, sir."

Flournoy said, "Then you do cash payroll checks from Flournoy Drilling here."

"Yes, sir," Salas said.

"How curious. Well, then. May I write out a check for $350?"

He slid the checkbook around in a small arch so Salas could see its printed face more easily. He recognized the last name on the check. His eyes went from the printed name to Flournoy's face.

"No, sir. I'm sorry," Salas wrote.

"My bad feeling got worse, but the gentleman remained composed. His pen went back to his breast pocket and the checkbook disappeared into his jacket.

"He looked right at me," he wrote.

"Interesting," Flournoy replied.

His voice was easy, the words drawn out smoothly. He had a slight grin on his face. But he was not ruffled in the least, Salas wrote.

"You will cash my company's checks, but you won't take my personal check.

Oh, well. Thank you."

Flournoy turned briskly and importantly on his heel and walked away, followed by the two that had flanked him. Neither ever spoke. Salas wrote that he went on about his business. The staff were busy.

"The next day the store manager, Jesse Salazar, called me over and asked me point blank. 'Did you refuse to cash a personal check yesterday for $500?'"

"Yes, sir. I followed policy," I said, cautiously.

"That was Lucien Flournoy." Jesse wasn't angry, but he wasn't happy either.

"I was just following store policy, sir," Salas wrote.

"Yes. That's right, and you should. Good. But if he ever comes in here again it's okay to cash his check for whatever amount."

"I don't have to call you, sir."

His boss said he did not have to call. Flournoy was probably one of a dozen people in that area wealthy and famous enough locally that he could get past the store rules on check-cashing. Way past. As the boss man told Salas, "for any amount..."

But the encounter showed Salas the kind of a man Flournoy was, still humble even with all his money and power. Still polite in public even if embarrassed a little when rebuffed by "the rules."

Flournoy certainly could readily display his natural good will toward others. It just wasn't in his nature to be deliberately cruel to anyone—especially a man just doing his job. But deep down, the morals and ethics and simple human decency he learned from his tough mother, stayed with him for life.

> *"If you think professionals are expensive, go hire an amateur and see how expensive things can really get." —Oilfield blowout specialist Red Adair*

Chapter 8

HE KNEW THE DRILL ALL-RIGHT

Almost seven million feet of "hole" were drilled by Flournoy and his crews between 1958 and 1977 in and around the million-acre King Ranch in South Texas. Flournoy had a contract to drill for Exxon—but in 1958 the company was named Humble Oil and Refining Company, the mega-oil monopoly that is now ExxonMobil.

"We SAFELY drilled the 1,000th well for Exxon in 1977, but just barely missed the seven-million-foot mark," Flournoy said. He'd had a sign built and erected with the words: WELL No. 1000. FLOURNOY DRILLING COMPANY IS DRILLING THE 1000th WELL FOR EXXON COMPANY, U.S.A.; 6,937,128 FEET OF HOLE. 1958 TO 1977.

"I was mighty proud of the achievement, and even more important was our safety record. No one was killed or maimed in getting the job done in that long period of time. But safety comes first with me in the oilfield, and always has as a drilling contractor," he said.

In fall 1958, Flournoy drilled his first well for Exxon, and "we had a real good run. Very good. During all that time there wasn't a loss of life or a permanent disabling accident. This is what I am especially proud of, along the path all over South Texas for Exxon. We have had problems but we always came out alright because I've always emphasized safety," he said.

"(It's) pretty tricky drilling down there but I had the very best people working for my company, of course, and we'd gotten into some discussions concerning the proper techniques to apply at a given time to control the unpredictable gas and oil zones down in this area … Exxon offered a program to teach control of gas 'kicks' by sending a contractor's and operator's rig personnel to a school where they can operate control equipment under simulated blowout conditions.

"If the controls are operated properly, the well will take the kick, control the pressures, and allow normal drilling to resume. And that's where close cooperation between the operator and some contractors makes for a long successful association. The contractors thought it was a good program," Flournoy said.

"Down here in this South Texas area it's sometimes necessary to use a drilling fluid weight in close balance, but slightly greater than normal expected pressure at target depth to protect a producing zone above the target zone. And, this procedure can sometimes allow a well to take a kick or try to blowout. Most of these kicks are controlled by the method taught at the Exxon training center," he said.

Much of Flournoy's equipment was of his own design—his ideas in the equipment configurations.

"The main object of the designs we've made are speed and safety. If a rig can be moved and ready to "spud" in two hours less time, more profits are earned the first day and the safety feature is important to profitability because the insurance premium cost is related to accidents," Flournoy said.

"In 1976, all 28 of our yard employees received a cash bonus and a banquet for going three years without a lost-time accident. That's more than 224,000 man-hours. During that time, we made 434 rig moves, built parts for and assembled two drilling rigs and three new trucks, and repaired and maintained all related equipment. We had eight drilling rigs, 16 heavy hauling trucks, nine pick-ups, 25 automobiles and two four-wheel-drive vehicles. And they all take a beating out there in the oil patch," Flournoy said, in a 1977 interview for the Alice Echo newspaper.

"The trucking department, with three 20-ton tandems, can move two 9,000- foot rigs in one day, or they can leave in the morning and be in the yard at noon after moving one rig. And they know how to do it quickly but safely," he said.

An article about Flournoy in a 1977 oilfield magazine "The Drilling Contractor" stated the 'rig in a rush' operation of Flournoy's began years before, when he contracted with Shell Oil Company, to drill 151 wells in the Big Foot area of South Texas.

"We drilled 515,339 feet of hole in 143 days using only two rigs. We were really punching them down. We didn't make much money but we got the bills paid and we learned some things about moving rigs quickly," Flournoy said.

According to the magazine, "Red West, Flournoy vice president and manager, testified to his company's talent at moving quickly: 'We really have it down.

When we're development-drilling, we've finished one well and been ready to spud on another in seven hours. Of course, the site was prepared but we keep the crews jumping hard when we want to get the job done.'"

The 1977 article stated: "And now, although Lou Flournoy keeps busy on a variety of civic organizations, state commissions and is a director on several boards, he still keeps close tabs on the company he formed with the first self-designed rig he put into operation 30 years ago ..."

In the article, Pete Peterson, Flournoy's vice president and general manager, said: "Lou challenges his men to find a better way to do each job for less money. Doing it for less money with today's inflationary pace would be setting a record itself."

Alice resident Dale Wilson spent some time working for Flournoy Drilling Company. He agreed to an interview by phone.

"(Flournoy) hired me as a roustabout and roughneck. He was a great guy— truly self-made. His generation is about gone—the so-called Greatest Generation—and when the last one is gone, we'll look back and realize those shoes are very tough to fill," Wilson said in the 2002 interview.

He explained in detail what it was like to set up a drilling rig in the vast Coastal Plains.

"You go out in a ranch and build a self-sufficient town, really. On the rig site you must have electricity, water, the equipment. It's just fascinating. You have to have an engine that runs 24-hours a day, digging a deep hole in the middle of the earth. You're always painting, especially if you're a roustabout—an unskilled worker—but everybody's got to stay up on the equipment. What really fascinated me were the trucks and how fast you can be set up somewhere and ready to go," Wilson said.

A lot of Flournoy's success could be traced back to one of his close associates Red West, who was highly competent in drilling operations—coordinating the work "like a traffic cop in downtown Manhattan," Wilson said, with a chuckle.

Flournoy would sit for hours with friends talking on the phone or in his office. One day a very successful oilman/geologist sat across from me, and his name was Charles Brocato. He was the first man—and in front my my boss—to really "tell you how to do an oil deal." And he spoke for a *good while*. I grasped the part about getting big money to drill a well. The other facts were hard to understand. But Flournoy hired me to write, not drill.

"Get at least 10 years' experience (after your geology degree) to know what the hell is going on. To fully function," Brocato said. "We'd get together, drilling contractors, etc., and get $40,000 together. One drilling contractor stole that money one night and ran off to Mexico. We never saw him again. The bank paid off, made a good well. Con-men are always a part of that life, or any other business," he said. "Here's how you put it together. I drilled a well on the Lower Frio, 10,000 feet, decades ago and it is still paying off. You get a deal, work mostly with logs and maps. Then put a lease together. Find some investors, then go to a small company or drill yourself with investors, in escrow, get a contract signed, a permit from the Texas Railroaded Commission, get your rig and spud in. The start drilling to total depth, then you run logs to see what you've got—hydrocarbons in the sand. Hopefully. Then you can case the hole, with logs and neutrons and gamma rays. Later, put a Christmas Tree railhead with your perforating gun, runnin' through the tubing. Then pray for good luck," Brocato said.

"Popularity never was what drove Mr. Flournoy. He had a vision, a dream, of what he wanted and he stuck by his guns, his convictions. He will take a tough stand, when necessary. When you see a guy like him, a mentor, when he speaks, he speaks with wisdom…," Wilson added. "You can clearly see by the longevity of his employees. You would see guys retire and yet they would still be working for him. In 1975, I was 18 and making $8 an hour, and (with overtime) sometimes $12 an hour. The reason I quit and went back to college was because I fell asleep going home from the rig one night, and almost had a bad wreck. I went through a stop sign, across a road, and skidded into a field.

And I got married, too, so that made me think more about the dangerous work I was doing."

He said Flournoy was an expert, by that time, and everybody knew it.

"He knew what was going on with the rig and drilling and was one of those people everybody knew you could go to with just about any issue," Wilson said. "It goes a lot deeper than the money. He is very generous, and that's part of his democratic nature. Money doesn't create mentors. People seek his counsel for wisdom. For 30 years, I've kind of been in awe of him, and Maxine is a jewel. It's been a unique team effort. And I can't think of any time working for him that I ever disagreed with him. He just had a lot of common sense and expertise to go with it, from years working his way from the bottom to the top."

> *"We cannot afford at this time, especially in these times, to forget the rock from which we are hewn. God must become bigger and more personal in our lives if we, as individuals and nations, are to conquer and solve the great problems that lie before us."*
>
> *---House Speaker Sam Rayburn, 1941, speaking before Congress.*

Chapter 9

Women Airforce Service Pilots logged 60 million miles in missions across the U.S. during World War II. But they lacked many of the benefits offered to others who served their country.

After the war, the women paid their own way home. Families of 38 of the women who died in the line of duty bore the costs of transporting their bodies home and the funerals.

It was 1977 before the women were granted status as veterans.

After her WASP service during World War II, Maxine said she "wrote to every address I could find to continue flying." And that's how she came to Alice, where she lived nearly 60 years. She landed a part-time commercial pilot job there in early 1945.

"They didn't pay me as much as they would a man," Maxine said. "But I was happy."

Among the reasons: the chance to take pilot instructor training at the Alice airport, where she met her future husband.

Lucien Flournoy was a petroleum engineer in 1945 for an Arkansas company that her boss' drilling company was working with.

"My boss asked if Lucien wanted to meet his pilot," she said. "He was surprised I was a gal, and he didn't waste much time asking me for a date."

They married a year later, and over the next 20 years raised three daughters, before she flew again.

In the mid-1960s, Lucien bought an airplane for a charter service he launched.

"While it was for the business, he told me it was mine," she said. "So, I called it mine whether it was or not."

She flew herself to annual Women Airforce Service Pilot reunions, until about 1985 when an oil field recession hit hard and to keep people on salary, Flournoy had to sell the airplane, she said.

She hasn't piloted a trip since. But even at almost 100 years old, if she had to do it, she could. She's a tough lady, with longevity and confidence in her genetic make-up.

"I was sorry to let it go," she said. "I had to take an airline flight to my next reunion, and it wasn't the same."

Maxine Edmondson joined the Civilian Pilot Training program while attending junior college in 1943 in her hometown of Joplin, Missouri.

"The rules said 10-percent (of the trainees) could be girls, so there were nine boys and me," said, with a laugh, remembering the details of her first encounters with the new flight program. "In July 1941, they cut all the girls out of the program, but in 1943 I was asked to join the WASP—and that stands for Women Airforce Service Pilots. I'd never heard of them. I was interviewed and was accepted, and was sent to Camp Crowder, in Neosho, Missouri. I went down there and got my physical and passed it, and pretty soon I was in Sweetwater, that's where almost everybody trained. I was 22-years-old in 1943, at that time, and it was Avenger Field in Sweetwater, Texas—West Texas."

Maxine first expressed her fondness for, and her desire to join the WASP training, in an Oct. 21, 1942 letter to Mrs. Nancy Harkness Love, commander of the "WAFS" (Women's Air Force Services): "Dear Mrs. Love, I have heard about the WAFS through newspapers, magazines, and newsreels, and am very much interested in joining it. I have inquired at the Army Air Corps recruiting office here several times but they have no information regarding it," she wrote, from her home near Joplin. "I have a private pilot certificate obtained through a primary CPT program. I realize this isn't much flying time but I hope it will help me to get into the WAFS. Would you please send me any information you may have that will tell me more about the WAFS (Women Airforce Ferry Squadron)? Thank you for your consideration. Yours truly, Maxine Flournoy."

Maxine Flournoy (recent)

In a letter dated Jan. 20, 1943, Maxine again expressed her strong interest in the flight program. She addressed the letter to Miss Jacqueline Cochran, director of the Women's Flying Training Headquarters, Flying Training Command, Texas and Pacific Building, Fort Worth, Texas:

"Dear Miss Cochran: My questionnaire for the Flying Training Command is enclosed. I realize that my flying experience is practically nothing, but I have been interested in getting into flying for a very long time. If I flew 20 hours very soon and brought my total up to 75 hours, could I be considered for an applicant and eligible for a personal interview with you? Thank you for your consideration. Yours very truly, Maxine Edmondson."

She also followed-up with a letter dated April 16, 1943, to Cochran. She was not about to take no for an answer, and that's clear enough. She aggressively pursued the program, a fact certainly not lost on the officials overseeing the training.

"In your letter of March 3, you stated that my name would be furnished a recruiting officer who would contact me when she is in the area. I am very anxious to make application and since no recruiting officer has yet been in this area, could I speed my application by making a trip to Fort Worth for an interview? If so, please tell me when I can be interviewed. Yours very truly, Maxine Edmondson."

Miss Cochran wrote Maxine back and told her to notify her when the potential trainee had logged 75 hours as a civilian pilot—which she certainly would go on to surpass.

Maxine said at the time, "I have had a primary C.P.T. (civilian pilot trainee) program at Joplin Municipal Airport. I have a total of 55 hours in Piper Cubs, also about 3 hours dual (twin engine) in a Fairchild '22', took the ground course with the C.P.T. which included some air regulations, meteorology navigation, and aerodynamics. I have had no instrument training. No accidents."

"The command was pretty full, and they were sending us to other places. Hondo (Rio Grande Valley) for navigation school, and sometimes we would fly to San Antonio. We were assigned to fly planes and the engines had to be revved-up and slowed down. We would fly around with a slow setting, and give different instrument readings. Mine was an open cockpit," Maxine said. "I had thought of it as being glamorous, with the scarf, etcetera, but the people would yell at you and you had to obey or you'd get washed-out. We didn't have good communications, and we wore a parachute. The engine training was at Hondo. We'd fly 1,000 miles at a time, at least, and we'd navigate with the sun as he headed over to California, and we'd navigate with the stars—celestial navigation—coming back at night. Sometimes, we'd get pretty far off course."

In March 2010, Maxine and other surviving WASP crew-women from World War II, were collectively awarded the Congressional Gold Medal by President Barack Obama (Obama signed the bill), and she attended the gathering and ceremony in Washington, D.C. That Gold Medal is the highest civilian award offered in the U.S.

That Medal is perennially housed in the Smithsonian, but all the WASP survivors received a bronze version of the Big Gold one.

Maxine then moved forward in advanced training at Hondo Army Air Corps Field—near Hondo, Texas. She may have trained further in

Florida—but she said "we flew all over the place, whether it was night or day."

WASPs did everything else their male-partners did except combat training. Once chosen as a WASP officer—after she completed that training--Maxine was transported by train to Hondo, Texas, Army base where she lived in the barracks with the other women pilots. She and other WASPs were sent to an officer training school in Orlando, Fla., when the group received the first Santiago blue uniforms issued to them along with the shoulder bag.

These were the first women to fly U.S. military aircraft and helped pave the way for women in the aviation field. After the WASP program disbanded, Flournoy was hired as a commercial pilot in Alice, Texas.

Best wishes to Carl Flores -

Carter

Carter on Air Force One

JIMMY CARTER
September 15, 1980

To Lucian Flournoy

I enjoyed seeing you today in Corpus Christi,
and was pleased you were able to travel with
me to Houston on Air Force One.

Your friendship and support will be very
valuable to me this year. Thank you!

Sincerely,

Jimmy

Mr. Lucian Flournoy
Post Office Box 1578
Alice, Texas   78332

We'll work together
on S. Texas —

Jimmy Carter Note

Former President Jimmy Carter appointed Flournoy to the World USO board, for which she attended meetings in many different countries.

The Congressional Gold Medal is an award bestowed by the United States Congress and is, along with the Presidential Medal of Freedom, the highest civilian award in the United States. A Congressional Gold Medal is created by the United States Mint to specifically commemorate the person and achievement for which the medal is awarded.

Maxine would often laugh remembering her time with the WASPs. That was a highly interesting and rewarding time of her young life, and it was the main factor that brought her and Lucien together not long after the end of World War II. Both had an interest in flying, in defense of their country, and their second daughter, Betty Lou, or "Boo", followed in Maxine's area of aerial interest while a student in the early 70s, at U.T. Austin.

She was a member of the Longhorns Flying Club, and Maxine was experienced enough to be her "teacher"—so she could get good advice when needed.

"The first time she went solo, she was a little shocked that there were other planes up there, she told me," Maxine said. "I told her that I always avoided weather when I could, though I later had an instrument rating, but I never liked flying through clouds. Years later, I would fly planes by myself to Cleveland, Ohio, Little Rock, Arkansas, Reno, Nevada, and would then land in Las Vegas."

Due to Flournoy's influence—his professional assistance and personal friendship with President Jimmy Carter, and U.S. Senator Lloyd Bentsen, on top of her valiant service during World War II—she was named to the national USO board.

"I was on the board four years and then joined the USO of South Texas. I am now a member emeritus, I guess that means you're just about to leave, doesn't it? We had dinner at Bob Hope's home in Palm Springs. He was sick with the flu, and we were sitting on the piano and he had a huge fireplace. We were all served a very nice dinner," Maxine said.

"We had Bob Hope all to ourselves. He posed me. I was just gonna stand there like I always do. He said, 'put your hand up to the cap.' That's how the photo happened, after he posed me. He knew how to do it."

Maxine said it was strange how she wound up in Alice at close to the same time her future husband would arrive.

"I was trying to find a flying job. A lot of WASPs were joining the reserves, or the National Weather Service, etc. I wrote to every aviation magazine, flying magazines, in search of a job. At that time, I didn't have an instrument rating, but Arthur Canales, at the (Alice) airport said I could work on my instrument rating from there. I got the job I'd applied for, a little airplane, and a little company, but at least I was in the air," she said. "The Alice airport and other small ones in the area such as the Orange Grove location, were U.S. Navy auxiliary fields with manned control towers 24-hours a day, but they were for the aviation trainees based at Naval Air Station Corpus Christi.

"You would be surprised when you got up there to altitude. You'd look around and not know north from south. I was headed to Galveston one time, and went out over the ocean, and lost my bearings. I wound up way off the shoreline. I wasn't scared or anything, but it was a little tense."

Maxine Edmondson was accepted into WASP training in a May 27, 1943 letter from General H.G. Hudgens, of the Army Air Forces Flying Training Command in Fort Worth, Texas. The letter ordered her to report at her own expense, "at 10 a.m., June 27, to the Commanding Officer, 318th AAF Contract Flying School (Women), Avenger Field, Sweetwater, Texas.

"Provisions have been made for your employment on Civil Service status at the rate of $150 per month during your satisfactory pursuance of flying instruction under Army control. Upon completion of the Army instruction course, and if physically qualified, you will be eligible for employment as a utility pilot at a rate of $250 per month, subject to your satisfactory performance of the duties assigned you," the letter from Gen. Hudgens states. "No allowance is made for your subsistence and maintenance during the term of this appointment. No uniform will be issued during the period of the training course."

On June 7th that year, Maxine would receive a telegram from headquarters in Fort Worth noting a change in reporting date—from June 27 to July 5—to the Avenger Field commanding officer.

"Bus will leave 0900 hours at the Bonnet Hotel Sweetwater for Avenger Field."

While she waited to start training, Maxine worked as a "grinder" for the Peerless Machinery Company in Joplin. She lived at the family home at Rural Route 1, Box, 517, Joplin, MO—out in Jasper County. She was earning 40-cents per hour starting wage, in July 1942, and when she quit to enter pilot training, she'd been bumped-up to 60-cents per hour. She would get about two years of college before "shipping out" for training-- from Sept. 1939 to Jan. 1942, at Joplin Junior College.

Before working at the machine shop, Maxine was a clerk and window decorator at the S.S. Kresge Dime Store in Joplin—from Dec. 1938 to July 1942—earning .23 cents per hour when she started, and 26 cents per hour when she quit that job for the machinery work.

In her WASP application, Maxine listed three references: H.E. Blaine, dean of the Joplin Junior College; B.A. Pugh, minister of the First Baptist Church in Joplin; and C.W. Poor, a medical doctor in Joplin.

Two days after receiving the telegram, and as requested, she acknowledged receipt of the message and noted her intention to be there on time as scheduled, and she did report as ordered.

She had to take a physical on May 10, 1943, just 22 years old, as a student pilot with the Army Air Corps, at the Camp Crowder Station Hospital in Missouri, and later at Avenger Field. The physical states that Maxine was almost 5 feet 6 inches tall, and weighed about 120 pounds—very physically and emotionally fit, and highly intelligent. An excellent pilot, as she would later prove, with a lot of good sense. By the time she entered WASP training in Sweetwater, she was already a good flier.

Though the WASPs were not viewed by the War Department as part of the U.S. military, all the women had to raise the right hand and take an "oath of office, affidavit, and declaration of appointee."

This oath states: "I, Mary Maxine Edmondson, do solemnly swear (or affirm) that I will support and defend the constitution of the United States against all enemies, foreign and domestic; that I will bear true faith and allegiance to the same; that I take this obligation freely, without any mental reservation or purpose of evasion; and that I will well and faithfully discharge the duties of the office on which I am about to enter. So help me God."

By Dec. 18, 1943, Maxine had successfully completed "the prescribed course of instruction under the Women's Pilot Training Program: and was authorized to fly military aircraft. That day she was directed to more extensive flight training at Hondo Army Air Field in the Texas Valley, with seven other young women: Adaline Blank, Elvira Griggs, Frances McInerney, Esther Mueller, and Lois Nash. She was fairly happy about the assignment location, not knowing that South Texas would one day be home for life.

Other training facilities were located at Marana Army Air Field, in Arizona; Lemoore Army Air Field, in California; Minter Army Air Field, in California; Gardner Army Air Field, in Taft, California; Chico Army Air Field, in California; Douglas Army Air Field, in Arizona; Williams

Army Air Field, in Arizona; Childress Army Air Field, in Childress, Texas; Maxwell Field, in Montgomery, Alabama; Scott Field, in Illinois.

"Above pilot trainees are granted ten (10) days annual accrued leave and will report to their new stations on 1 January 1944 ...," according to the letter, signed by Captain J.C. Ward, of the U.S. Army Air Corps adjutant general's office.

"...in lieu of subsistence, a flat per diem of six dollars ($6.00) per day is authorized for period of travel only, in accordance with existing law and regulations," states a Dec. 18, 1943 communique from Captain J.W. Ward, to the trainees.

As of Jan. 1, 1944, Maxine listed her address as: "WASP, Hondo Air Field, Barracks 1602, Room 4, Hondo, Texas." She was earning about $250 per month, or $3,000 per year for the highly demanding and often dangerous work.

Two days later, she received a letter from Lt. John Storin, Army Air Corps personnel officer, Civilian Section: "MEMORANDUM: The following named Woman Civilian Pilot is reporting to this station (Hondo Army Air Field, Army Air Force Navigation School) for assignment: Mary Maxine Edmondson. She will report to the following offices and then report back to the Civilian Personnel Office—provost marshal, intelligence officer, civilian war housing, director of training, post operations, flight surgeon's office, public relations, and pilot transitional training."

At that time, Jan. 1944, Maxine was certified as an AT-7 (training plane) copilot. The AT-7 was a (describe). She was part of the 86th training group. By that time, she'd been awarded the Emblem for Civilian Service—a medal reflecting her commitment and skill.

By June 1944, while at Hondo Field, Maxine was temporarily assigned with two other female trainees to report not later than 20 June 1944 to Army Air Force Tactical School in Orlando, Florida. She was accompanied by Mary Burke, and Frances Warms.

By that summer, Maxine had 629 hours flying time with the Army Air Corps, or WASP training, and 58 hours as a civilian pilot. On June 30, 1944, a day all the trainees were praying to reach, Maxine received a special order from Captain F.L. Dannelly, of the Army Air Corps adjutant's office:

"VOCO authorizing the following named WASPs to fly military aircraft after having completed the required courses of training are confirmed and made of record," Dannelly wrote. On that day, Maxine was a military trained pilot ready for stateside action. She was one of 48 young women in the same group who would be flying as WASPs. Her superior officer's report on Maxine, dated September 1944, listed her performance as "90-percent" or "very good."

The only injury-accident encountered by Maxine, according to her WASP file, was on October 1, 1944, when she was a passenger in a vehicle that crashed at the base, injuring her. According to the medical record, she sustained wounds.

The base doctor's report states: "Sunday, AM about 0215 (Oct 1, 1944) was sitting in right side of front seat of car, asleep, and apparently the driver went to sleep and ran into fence southeast corner of Hondo Army Air Field, Hondo, TX—were returning to field, driving west on road—patient does not remember what she hit because she was asleep, she was awakened rather rudely by the crash, and came on to hospital by car that drove by …

"…multiple, mild, bridge of nose, ½ cm in length, anterior aspect, right knee, 1 cm in length and dorsal surface, right foot, 1 and ½ inches in length. Contusion, moderate, lower lip; 1 and 1 accidentally incurred when car in which WASP was riding as a passenger ran off the road and struck corner post of fence, 1 October 1944 near Hondo Army Air Field, Hondo, Texas. 1 October 1944: operation. Suture of wounds. Anesthetic, local; 1-percent procaine. Time intervening, 30-minutes. Discharged from station hospital, 8th October 1944."

Maxine was 23 when she was involved in the car wreck. Her chart states she was 5 feet, six inches, tall; suffered typhoid, and had a tonsillectomy.

Maxine was first assigned to active duty with the 318th Army Air Force Flying Training Detachment at Sweetwater earning $1800 per year. She was a war Service appointment and that meant her service period was indefinite. Monthly room and board were a mere $28.60, and a quarter per uniform for cleaning and pressing. In Dec. 1943, she took 11 days annual leave and went back to Joplin for the holidays. At that time, her father—a Joplin dentist—lived at 1502 Main Street, in that Missouri town. Her mother, Ruth Wise lived at 1415 S. Catalina, in Los Angeles, CA.

On Nov. 24, 1944, Maxine satisfactorily completed the WASP Instrument Pilot Course, at Hondo. In that report, she is listed as having a daily average grade of 92-percent correct in the ground school but it wasn't easy for her to complete the course.

"Student basic flying at first very weak but showed rapid progress … student's general flying technique, judgment and procedures very good. Beam bracketing and recognizing of signals both on rate group and full panel were slightly above average," according to Erwin E. Ives, a flight instructor.

At age 23, after serving in the WASPs honorably, Maxine was discharged—or deactivated—Dec. 18, 1944 from the Hondo base. She had 837 hours of flying time.

She was qualified to fly solo in both single and multi-engine planes on Dec. 18, 1943, at Hondo Field. These were known as the PT-19, a 175-horsepower plane, and the AT-17, with 225-horsepower; the AT-6 with 650-horsepower, and the AT-7 with 450 horsepower.

Her instrument card was issued Nov. 22, 1944.

"…the above-named applicant is officially qualified to serve as first pilot …," wrote Col. Charles Dowman, Commanding Officer at Hondo Field.

Maxine said before college she never even imagined she'd ever get to fly airplanes. In those days, few women ever did that sort of thing: "I had no idea. Somebody asked me if I wanted to fly in the CPT Program (Civilian Pilot Training), and they said 10-percent could be girls. Nine boys and … me. This was before Pearl Harbor, July 1941, and I was asked to join up. I'd never even heard of them. Well, we got four gallons of gas per month to fly."

Maxine's last day of active duty is listed in her WASP file as Dec. 20, 1944, and the WASP program, training and active-duty, was deactivated on Jan. 24, 1945. While these brave women flew the same planes that men did during the war, and often in deadly conditions, performing an essential service for the U.S. war effort, they were not afforded veterans status, by the War Department, or President Franklin D. Roosevelt. His wife, First Lady Eleanor Roosevelt, must surely have taken more than a passing interest in honoring the WASPs with the veterans' status.

Maxine was featured in the Feb. 25, 2016 edition of Wingspan, the weekly publication of Naval Air Station Corpus Christi: " … (Maxine Flournoy) is among an elite group of women aviators, the first women in history to fly America's military aircraft. They are true trailblazers for those who would follow decades later ... and it was an accomplishment her own children didn't discover until more than three decades later."

Maxine Edmondson was born March 30, 1921 in the town of Wheaton, Missouri, populated by about 300 people, counting herself and family. When people went on summer vacation at the same time, the population would dwindle to about 200 people—a lonely midwestern village. Today, Wheaton has about 700 people. Her parents were from Stella, Missouri— her father was a dentist, and her mother tended to home life.

"We stayed in Stella until they divorced when I was only about 12 years old," Maxine said in a previous interview for this biography. "Then my mother moved us all to Columbus (Kansas)."

Due to her youth, and family situation, the "Roaring 20s" and the Great Depression, didn't affect Maxine as much as it did Lucien and his family.

"Nothing really stands out about that time, but we didn't have anything else to compare it to ... I just grew up at that time, and it seemed normal to us. We didn't go hungry. We had a roof, and didn't suffer too much, not really. We had a pretty normal life, though he were definitely not wealthy," Maxine said, laughing a little bit. " ... it's just how things were, so it wasn't odd to me. My mother would try to feed people, the unemployed and the hobos, who would stop by and ask for a little something to eat. That was just how things were at the time," she said.

"It was very good and very thorough," she said, of the WASP program.

The women pilots would fly the Fairchild PT-19, the BT-15 Valiant and the T-6 Texan. These were the same planes and training for American men at that time, a duration of about six months.

"It was exciting. I was flying ... and that's what I wanted to do. I liked everything about it," she said.

Though a vital project, many Americans at that time scoffed at the idea of women being on active-duty instead of "in the kitchen, where we belonged," Maxine said, rolling her eyes.

"Not everybody supported the WASP program."

During roughly two years as an active-duty WASP flier, Maxine flew trainers, but also the B-26 bomber—a highly difficult plane to fly safely.

"I was (at Hondo) until the end of my time. I was thrilled to complete the long-distance graduations flights normally routed from Hondo to Los Angeles.

My mother had relocated there, so I was able to visit her on those flights," she said.

In the summer of 2016, Maxine remained philosophical about her WASP service even as she made an initial approach on her 100th birthday. WASP personnel were not treated the same as male pilots, though they did dangerous flying and an essential service for our nation during wartime.

"The military needed women flying planes to give an extra motivation for young male pilot trainees, I suppose. I think we were good motivators," she said. "(The military) used us for psychological purposes. An example is the B-26, a bomber, and male pilots were afraid of it … they called it the 'flying coffin.' So, we would be ordered to check-out on the B-26, to fly it, and then the plane was sent on to the B-26 transition school.

"They would then line up all of the male cadets on the flight line to await the arrival of some VIPs. So, in comes the B-26 … and the only people who would get out were WASPs. Then men were so shocked, they would say: Well, by God, is a woman can fly it, then we men can too!" Maxine chuckled.

Some of the best years in her life were spent as a WASP— intensely-packed events like time in high school or college, and remembered and revered forever. But as World War II was drawing out toward a rather rapid end, Maxine was dismayed in December 1944 when the government ended the WASP training and operations.

"They did away with our program; it didn't pass the Senate. They disbanded us after that – before the war was over. It really was a bad deal for us."

WASPs, regardless of their often perilous and sometimes deadly duties, and the vital role they played, were not granted veterans status so these brave young women could not go to Veterans Administration hospitals, nor could they receive an education through the G.I. Bill.

"WASPs killed in the line-of-duty weren't allowed burial expenses, or to even be buried with the U.S. flag draped over their coffin," she said.

Only 38 out of a total 1,102 female pilots in the World War II WASP training/operations were killed; 11 during training accidents, and 27 in the line-of-duty.

After the war, Maxine wouldn't have to wait long to get back into the air. Sometime in 1945, she was hired to pilot a plane for a Houston-based oilfield equipment company with an office in Alice.

"With the company, I flew all over Texas and parts of Oklahoma. I was able to get some good use out of my training" she said, smiling. "I was able to obtain a commercial rating, and multiple-engine rating, with the WASPs."

After her first child arrived, named Mary Anne, in May 1949, Maxine put her piloting time on-hold to held pitch in and raise a family and help Lucien's flourishing oil drilling business as a dutiful house body. But after the kids were old enough, she would find a way to fly again, with the help of her often-accommodating husband.

"Lucien bought a plane—a Cessna 337--for me, finally," she said. "But it's funny, he never liked to fly with me ... he always said I was an excellent pilot, to anybody who would listen, but he didn't like giving up control to anybody— especially me," she said.

Lucien and Maxine yielded three children in their 57 years together: Mary, Betty Lou, and Helen.

Even her own kids had no idea what she did during World War II because she never talked about it much, and the government ordered all WASP records sealed for 35 years after the end of the war. In 1977, the records were unsealed, during the Carter Administration.

"The people in World War II never talked about it with their children. The children never heard anything about it, really, until the grandchildren started hearing about it in school. We never heard of WASPs," Mary Anne (Flournoy) Guthrie said, in a 2016 interview:

"... (WASP) wasn't in textbooks. So, here we are, in our retirement years, and all of a sudden – they (women pilots) are 'famous.' But when we were growing up, they weren't ... she started flying a lot when I was in high school. Once she started flying again, my dad always had her in airplanes – and they were always twin-engines," Guthrie said.

According to the 2016 "Wingspan" article: "More than three decades after her service, in 1977, President Jimmy Carter signed legislation granting full military status for the WASPs, and he appointed Maxine to the USO board of directors that same year.

"In 1984, the members of the WASP program were awarded the World

War II Victory Medal, and those who served more than one year were awarded the American Theater Ribbon/American Campaign Medal ... Maxine would later serve as president of the WASP Association—from 2000 to 2002," the article stated. "Later, in July 2009, President Barack Obama signed legislation awarding the WASP members the Congressional Gold Medal—the nation's highest civilian award. Maxine was among those who traveled to Washington in March 2010 to receive the award."

Not long before this manuscript was completed, Maxine's daughters and grandkids were planning to celebrate her 99th birthday—March 30, 2020. Never a person to helplessly give-in to age or sit around and "remember the good ole days" she did admit, in one of our interviews, that the Congressional medal was quite a surprise. And the greatest honor she ever received.

"We didn't know at that time that we were breaking new ground for women ... we paved the way for all of them. We have reunions with them—today's female military pilots— and they come up and thank us for paving the way for them.

I guess we did ... I encourage (female trainees) to continue. Even if it is really hard, just go ahead and do it," she said.

"Failure is not an option" –Gene Kranz, NASA Flight Director Apollo 13

Chapter 10

Fidel at NASA

I met Fidel Rul, a native resident of Alice, in the summer of 1997 while covering some stories for area newspapers and working as a correspondent for the much-larger San Antonio Express-News—a couple of hours north by car or bus—or for the brave-at-heart, you might take a freight train if you can find an open car—like Flournoy used to do, and even Rul said in the early 1950s, hitch-hiking across America was considered fairly safe and widely accepted.

Fidel Rul paratrooper

Flournoy's assistance to Fidel in the early days, when he was a struggling student at Texas A & M University at College Station, was critical. Many white people would not hire Mexican-American boys like Fidel, no matter how smart and hard-working they may have been—and the Mexican boys usually were. So, Flournoy knew this young man was bound for something special in life, based on his grades, his team spirit, his commitment to work, and so he hired him every summer at top wages so Fidel could earn enough money and attend Texas A & M.

He would graduate with a B.S. degree, and later was hired as an engineer to work on the brand new intercontinental ballistic missile (ICBM) program that would for the first time in history be capable of delivering a high-yield hydrogen bomb by missile within 30 minutes to the heart of what was then—in the Cold War—known as the U.S.S.R., or the Union of Soviet Socialist Republics.

"When I was growing up in Alice, I certainly could not have even imagined, John, and no one could, that I would one day play a key role in helping three American astronauts make it to the moon, with the first two men in human history to step foot on the lunar surface," Rul said. "During the course of my 32-year career as a NASA engineer, I became a main player in the Lunar Landing project of 1969, a quest President Kennedy predicted in 1962 to become 'the greatest accomplishment in the history of mankind.'"

Rul lamented lack of chances for young Latin-Americans to succeed, as he did: "The biggest problem for (Latinos) seeking this type of position is that many of us come from a different type of environment. Our goals are extremely low, and we don't feel that we have the capacity to do the work. We often reject ourselves first. One you jump in the middle of applying yourself, and have confidence in yourself, the doors are open."

Moon Shot Flight Director Gene Kranz worked with Rul, a lot. He said: "Fidel was a key man in our Apollo program."

Though later on, when Apollo 13 did not achieve its main objective of landing men on the moon again, to Kranz its astronauts' rescue is an example of the "human factor" born out of the 1960s space race. According to Kranz, this factor is what is largely responsible for helping put America on the Moon in only a decade. The blend of young intelligent minds working day in and day out by sheer willpower yielded "the right stuff."

Kranz had this to say about the "human factor":

"They were people, like Fidel, who were energized by a mission. And these teams were capable of moving right on and doing anything America asked them to do in space," he said.

"The Kranz Dictum" as it became widely known among key NASA personnel, could have been called "The Flournoy Dictum" too. It demanded 100-percent effort all the time—not just some of the time. There was no room for oversights or stupid mistakes.

Rul knew most, if not all, of the main NASA astronauts from all three major orbital missions: Mercury, Gemini, and Apollo. One NASA employee recalled that Kranz called a meeting of his branch and flight control team on the Monday morning following the Apollo 1 disaster that killed astronauts Gus Grissom, Ed White, and Roger Chaffee. Kranz made the following address to the gathering (explaining The Kranz Dictum), in which his expression of values and admonishments for future spaceflight are his legacy to NASA:

"Spaceflight will never tolerate carelessness, incapacity, and neglect. Somewhere, somehow, we screwed up. It could have been in design, build, or test. Whatever it was, we should have caught it. We were too gung-ho about the schedule and we locked out all of the problems we saw each day in our work. Every element of the program was in trouble and so were we. The simulators were not working, Mission Control was behind in virtually every area, and the flight and test procedures changed daily. Nothing we did had any shelf life. Not one of us stood up and said, "Dammit, stop!" I don't know what Thompson's committee will find as the cause, but I know what I find. We are the cause! We were not ready! We did not do our job. We were rolling the dice, hoping that things would come together by launch day, when in our hearts we knew it would take a miracle. We were pushing the schedule and betting that the Cape would slip before we did," he stated forcefully.

"From this day forward, Flight Control will be known by two words:

"Tough" and "Competent". *Tough* means we are forever accountable for what we do or what we fail to do. We will never again compromise our responsibilities. Every time we walk into Mission Control, we will know what we stand for. *Competent* means we will never take anything for granted. We will never be found short in our knowledge and in our skills. Mission Control will be perfect. When you leave this meeting today you will go to your office and the first thing you will do there is to write "Tough and Competent" on your blackboards. It will *never* be erased. Each day when you enter the room these words will remind you of the price paid by Grissom, White, and Chaffee. These words are the price of admission to the ranks of Mission Control," he said.

The Saturn V rocket, used in the Apollo 11 Moon landing, weighed 6.2 million pounds fully fueled, and generated 7.6 million pounds of thrust at lift-off. The main fuel on take-off was from petroleum—it was kerosene. That apparently provided the rocket with enough initial thrust to achieve escape velocity and thereby go into orbit, before heading out into deep space toward the lunar surface, Rul said, as he explained more about his own life experiences in Alice.

Apollo 11 crew quarantined

Rul started life the son of the town barber—an honest and honorable man. So, money was tight. He was proud of his family and his Latino heritage, and was determined to work however hard it took to succeed in getting that all-important B.S. degree.

"Two generations of (my family) fought with the armies of Pancho Villa during the northern Mexico civil war of the early 20th century," Rul said, displaying an old photo for me. "See the boy on the left? That's my father, Fidel Rul Sr., at the age of fourteen. On the right is my grandfather, Jesus Rull—the spelling of our name before the family left Mexico for the U.S. The picture was taken in 1916 at Atlisco de las Flores, Puebla, Mexico."

In that photo, NASA used in a newsletter about Rul, the boy and the father are both wearing bandoliers loaded with rifle cartridges, in peasant garb, standing at attention holding rifles.

"My grandfather was shot by a Mexican soldier, in front of my father, who struggled terribly after that and made his way to Alice," Rul said.

"He became a barber, and in the 1940's opened his own barbershop where my brother and I shined shoes and swept the floor. My parents' primary goal was to ensure that we obtained a proper education and pursue a viable career. Working for the Magnolia Oil Company and Mr. Flournoy's oil drilling company during the summers enabled me to complete my college education," Rul said.

"After graduating from the Texas, A&M University, I served in the US Army as an Infantry/Paratrooper Officer, and upon completion of my military obligation, I was hired as a Logging Engineer with an oil well service company based in Houston, Texas. While serving in this capacity, I traveled from east Texas to Louisiana off-shore drilling activity, back to south Texas, to Santa Ana, California, and finally to the Los Angeles area. It was during this time that I decided to seek employment in the aerospace industry, and I was hired immediately as a Research Engineer in the Minuteman Intercontinental Ballistic Missile (ICBM) Program. During the three years I worked with North American Aviation, I gained knowledge in the computer industry that greatly enhanced my professional profile. My application to join NASA received a positive respond, and my wife Emilia and I traveled across the country to the Goddard Space Flight Center in Greenbelt, Maryland.

"As a Computer Engineer, my initial assignment was to plan for the implementation and integration of computer systems with the data processing and telecommunications systems designated for NASA's worldwide space tracking network. NASA was in the process of establishing additional tracking stations around the globe for the purpose of providing communication between orbiting space crafts and the Mission Control Center in Houston, Texas. My responsibilities in this capacity continued to increase, and as a result I became part of the management team," Rul said.

"As the Mission to the Moon Program came to an end and as the Space Shuttle Program started, I had a strong desire to manage a NASA tracking station. My wish was realized when my boss designated me as Deputy Director of the California Tracking Station followed by assignments as Director of the Guam Tracking Station and then Director of the Hawaii Tracking Station. This book on the life of Mr. Flournoy was of great interest to me since I was personally familiar with Mr. Flournoy having met him in 1953 just before I started my college career at Texas A&M University.

"I continued to maintain close contact with Mr. Flournoy during these years since he would hire me any time I had a break from college. Following my retirement from NASA he was my strongest supporter when I decided to run for Alice Councilmember and then for Mayor. Mr. Flournoy's generous attributes were demonstrated annually with his significant contributions to local charities and the private and religious schools in our community. This story about an individual who came to South Texas with few assets but certainly with extremely high expectations and achieving the goals as documented by the author may even be categorized as a "rags to riches" venture, although "rags" might be a little farfetched," Rul said.

Ever the class-act, after he retired as director of the Goddard (tracking station) in Hawaii, he wrote a letter for all employees printed in the December 1989 edition of the base newspaper: "As a former station director of Hawaii, I welcome the opportunity to express my sincere appreciation and pay tribute to one of my favorite places in the NASA community," he wrote.

"The Hawaii Tracking Station has been one of the key supporting facilities of NASA's global network," he wrote. "(When Neil Armstrong) said 'one small step for a man' (that) was made possible by each and every one of you, and the steps taken in the future, will be because of you …"

"Flournoy has all the innocence of a Molotov cocktail"--Oilman Tubby Weaver.

CHAPTER 11

So, reluctantly, Flournoy finally sold his drilling company in 1997, after 50 years of highly profitable business, to a large company in Houston, but he kept a fast-paced business life with his production company for the next six years—until his death. He made a lot of money on that, too. Maybe as much as the one thousand wells he drilled as an Exxon drilling contractor. Or maybe a lot more. No one can say for sure. He may have been worth half a billion dollars, for all anyone knew.

His longtime buddy, Tubby, believed in Flournoy.

"He's got so many things going on, it's hard to say, but he's savvy. He's one hell of a business man. But he's honest, and he truly cares about his employees and their safety. To him, safety comes before everything else, and the workers, they know that," Weaver said, in a 2002 interview at his home in Corpus Christi.

Flournoy would take good care of his men, at all times, or he'd have his second-in-command, Red West, help him in that way. West worked for Flournoy many years in several capacities.

"Once you worked for Flournoy, you didn't want to work for anybody else," Weaver said. "He also paid top wages, so that was also a good incentive."

At an early age his grandpa helped the young Tubby start a cattle and hog operation on their old home place.

"I was only six years old," Tubby said, with his wide, toothy smile, and a slight South Texas accent—a variation on the West Texas drawl. "I milked cows and sold (the milk) to people and businesses around home—cafes, places to eat."

Six years later, in 1921, the boy had a herd of about 50 head of cattle, and about 50 hogs, he said. But that was a temporary occupation for Tubby. And fate probably played a big part in what would become his life's work as a geologist, an oilman.

In a November 2004 memorial article about Tubby, printed by the American Association of Petroleum Geologists Bulletin, Corpus Christi resident Ray Govett remembered Tubby's life: "(the) Luling-Branyon oil field was discovered in August 1922. Vernon Woolsey was the geologist for Edgar B. Davis, the man credited with discovery of the field. Woolsey showed Tubby The outcrop of the fault that traps hydrocarbons in the field into the bank of San Marcos River near Luling. This whetted Tubby's appetite for geology and (finding) oil," Govett wrote. "When Tubby was a little older, he helped survey, and clear, well locations in Luling and other nearby oil fields.

The Weaver family owned a home about a mile north of downtown Corpus Christi on the famed North Beach, where the family would spend summers On Corpus Christi Bay fishing, boating, swimming, laying in the sun, and Fine dining at the Nueces Club—the place for Corpus Christi's elite to meet.

"I was just barely 10 years old and we'd left the beach house a day or two before, when the 1919 Hurricane (name) blew our nice house away. We sure hated that, and I didn't go back until I took a job in summer 1927 right there in Corpus Christi, and that got me started in the oil business," Tubby said, in an early 2004 interview, at age 95, shortly before his death from the maladies of old age and years of hard work in the rugged, unforgiving, South Texas oilfields. "I was basically a driver for land men with Smith-Clark Oil Company. That got me into the business."

Tubby enrolled in fall 1927 at the University of Texas at Austin, focusing on Geological studies. In his first semester, he was nicknamed "Tubby" because his roommate, a varsity football player for the Longhorns, was called "Tuffy."

"I guess what it was is my friends figured I ought to have a name, too, a nick-Name like my roomie's," he said, laughing.

"It's funny too, because people called me that from then on, until today."

After completing all the required geology courses to get his degree, he still had A lot of other courses to complete, so he took a break from college to help an Uncle in the East Texas oil fields—where an underground ocean of oil called The Black Giant was discovered by a wildcatter named Dad Joiner, near Kilgore, Texas.

The Great Depression was in full-swing, and that hurt his uncle's business, so Tubby went back to college in 1932 received his B.S. in geology from U.T.

CHAPTER 12

THE DEAN OF SOUTH TEXAS DRILLING

The Exxon contract in 1958 was when the money really started rolling in for Flournoy Drilling Company, but in 1973 during the oil crisis, he got another big boost from the high oil prices. This came after years of struggling for Flournoy and most independent drilling/production companies.

Due to gradually increased importation of foreign oil, rig count in the U.S. began declining in 1955 and hit a low in 1970-71, while Americans were using even more petroleum products than ever, especially gasoline for automobiles. A lot of people were commuting from suburbs to the city, during that time— the period of massive urban flight. Cars made it easy to live far from work, so gasoline was in high demand. But by the early 1970s cutbacks among oil producing countries like Saudi Arabia, Venezuela, and Iran, among others, drove prices in the U.S. way up. This was bad for consumers, but good for people like Flournoy. At that time, electric utility companies began switching from coal-fired electric generating plants, to oil. Some of this would come from Libya and Nigeria, as well—where they produced low-Sulphur crude oil.

Coal generating plants power many U.S. cities, and contribute to a lot of pollution like mercury, pumped into the atmosphere, and that winds up in the oceans—and gets into big fish like tuna. Some people have claimed mercury poisoning from eating too much tuna—and that seems plausible, or even likely.

"So, oil and gas are much better solutions for power than coal, and you can see the evolution of that in ships and trains especially—coal to diesel," Flournoy said.

The American *energy crisis* truly started in 1971 by rapid growth in demand, shortage of supply, and also price controls imposed by the Nixon Administration as part of the president's anti-inflation efforts and it had the effect of discouraging domestic oil production while encouraging consumption. These controls created artificially low prices while discouraging both exploration for new oil and conservation of existing supplies.

Economic advisors generally believed the Nixon government should reduce the growth rate of consumption, raise domestic production, and develop a policy of importing oil only from secure areas—but none of those steps were taken by the Administration.

In 1970, the U.S. imported 3.2 million barrels per day, and in 1972 that rose to 4.5 million barrels per day. By 1973, the U.S. imported 6.2 million barrels per day, and independent refineries in the U.S., Europe and Japan began buying oil in a panic that sent prices soaring. When market prices exceeded the official posted prices, it signaled the end of a 20-year oil surplus—or glut— that kept prices low.

Between 1970 and 1973, the price for crude doubled, and other exporting countries collectively decided to take advantage of their uniquely profitable situation—they had America "over a barrel" and there was no way to deny it. Libya led the charge for a more equitable system so oil producing countries could get a larger cut of the profits from big oil companies. Oil was a weapon used by oil producing and exporting countries (OPEC) in an attempt to secure strategic regional objectives, and to get top dollar. In the late 1960s and early 70s, the U.S. still had plenty of oil reserves in Texas, Louisiana, and Oklahoma, but once America hit 100-percent of its production capability, as it did in the early 70s, that sharpened the blade of OPEC's weapon.

"There's two big things that happened after the Arab oil embargo of 1973— one was the natural gas shortage that occurred, and big policy action concerning natural gas. That new policy on natural gas affected Flournoy's life a lot more," said former Texas Governor Bill White, who served as deputy secretary of energy under President Jimmy Carter.

White and Flournoy were longtime personal and political friends when I interviewed him for this biography.

"I think it seems like I've known Lou Flournoy about all my life. He was always active politically in South Texas and he was helpful to me when I began to run for governor," White said. "He was one of my earliest supporters. When everybody said I had no chance, that it was likely to ruin my career—and I talked to a lot of people all over the state—Lou said, 'Mark, it'll be a tough race but I will support you.' I don't think at the time any of us knew how expensive it would be. Some of the people we counted on didn't come through, and it turned into a tough financial problem that got even tougher. He could have walked, buy Flournoy didn't. When that situation occurred, he said *I will support Mark* and he got energized. He was there to make up the difference in the campaign—with money and a company plane, a King Aire, he loaned me," White said. "He had faith and confidence in me. I don't think we would have won without him. He was very helpful. We needed a plane badly, and he came through at the most critical time. Our friendship started way before that, so I was no stranger to him."

White said he knew Flournoy had a lot of common sense, and excellent political judgment.

"And he has spent a lot of his time and money on the little guy. He is a guy who can become the glue that holds it all together," he said. "In a lot of cases, money ruins people but in Flournoy's case I think it made him a better man."

White said an old law passed by Congress during President Franklin D. Roosevelt's New Deal--regulating monopolies--subjected independent gas producers from the 1950s to the 1980s to very difficult conditions.

"There was a mistaken impression that the gas pipelines were monopolies and the law was designed to regulate monopolies ... as a result, the price set from the mid-1950s to the mid-1980s was usually below the cost of producing natural gas, so that during much of the time that Flournoy was a driller, natural gas was only a biproduct of trying to find oil," White said.

In the Corpus Christi and Alice areas, bright flames at the top of tall towers still stand as evidence that natural gas is often flared off, as the oil people call it, especially if it's second-rate gas. But you never see people deliberately burning off crude oil coming out of the ground.

"In 1975, there was a Texas congressman named Bob Krueger. I was his legislative assistant and had written about this problem in the mid-70s. I didn't even know anybody in the oil and gas industry at that time but I thought that the U.S. ought to be producing more natural gas, since it was a national emergency. We started legislation that resulted in a change of the law to create a free market for natural gas produced in the field. That occurred in 1979, and as a result of that, by the end of the 1970s and into the early 80s, you saw for the first time an explosion of drilling for gas. And we found a lot of it," he said.

"I think probably no one is alive on planet Earth today who has personally been involved in the drilling of oil and gas wells more than Lucien Flournoy and his crews. They were very productive. He has been involved in the drilling of more wells than are in the Middle East ... and he wouldn't 'stack up' (leave them rusting in the yards) his rigs. He would get more feet drilled every year than anyone else in the business," White said. "He understood how to price services, where to get used parts, how to get the most out of people, and it's honestly very high-tech dealing with geologists. You have to stay up with it, and he always has. I think there's a lot of people who, once they build a company up, play at the golf course. But the work takes place in the fields.

After he would get off work, after about 8 p.m., Flournoy would go back to the office and look at the drilling reports."

When Flournoy Drilling Company started operations throughout South Texas and the Rio Grande Valley, the Persian Gulf was still a backwater area and few had ever heard of Alaska's North Slope or even offshore drilling— definitely not deep-water drilling. In those days there were two major drilling areas—the West Texas Permian Basin and the South Texas-Gulf Coast region. Flournoy liked being where the action was.

As his company developed and grew in size, Flournoy could have easily picked up and moved to a larger city or to other drilling areas, but he never did. He chose to keep his headquarters in quiet and remote little Alice, and his presence there helped keep oilfield service companies in town. He was a major employer in the area for decades and at one time was the largest employer of all in Jim Wells County—with Alice being the seat of county government.

"He always managed to survive at a time when many others were going out of business," said Tavo Salinas, a Flournoy friend. "He kept his employees on the payroll, the biggest percentage of employees in the city. He had many rigs going, and 90-percent of his workers were out of Alice, and by keeping his rigs going he contributed to the people tied to the oil industry. This got the oil services companies to stay, welding shops, machine shops. He was a big reason they never left town."

To sum it up: if Flournoy had pulled out of Alice after he'd built up the company, the city's economy would've had a heart attack with no relief in sight. He always saw that "Greenwood" side of Alice—the pastoral, quieter and more neighborly way of life. He loved that aspect of the town, and the trusting network of loyal friendships a person can only really know in small towns and rural communities.

But staying in Alice was sometimes almost impossible. Flournoy had to weather the difficulties of competing against massive forces of nature and the economy, and his survival largely depended on being as wily and tough as a coyote—foraging for good tools and drilling equipment at cut-rate prices.

"We met through the oilfield auction in San Antonio," said Dan Kruse, founder of Superior Auctioneers and Marketing in San Antonio—the world's largest oilfield auctioning company with about $1 billion in sales from 1984 to the time Flournoy hired me to write his life story. A period of about 17 years.

"Lou (Flournoy) would come to our auction sales and buy good equipment at used prices and save a lot of money versus going to big dealers for new equipment. We helped a lot of drilling contractors save a lot of money during the 'down-time' of the 1980s. They could save fifty percent or more over retail sales by getting equipment at the auction, most of the time. I think that was one of the keys of his survival ... by spending a lot less he could bid less on a job and always outperform the competition," Kruse said.

"Some independent companies bought from us more than others. Lou even would speculate on some things. He bought drill pipe when it was really cheap and then he'd sell it off later and make a good profit. He always had integrity in his dealings. He always paid for what he bought and would always remove it from the yard when he said he would," Kruse said. "He and I became friendly as we shared our ideals of life—we both have faith in God and an understanding of the importance of forgiveness and good will, and how that helps people get along a lot better in life … he had the right ideals, goals and aspirations, and had an excellent character to try and reach those. He wasn't perfect, I'm not saying he was, but he was a man of integrity in my dealings with him when he owned the drilling company.

"As an example of how much people could save going through us, one time we sold Lou a rig where he went with us out to New Mexico to look at this oil well rig and he didn't pay a lot of money for it, either. He paid $450,000 on this rig.

At today's prices it would be around $6 million," he said, in the 2002 interview. "A brand new 20,000-foot rig would cost about $14 million today, and a used rig in good condition can be had for about $5 million."

One woman, who asked not to be named, said her father worked for Flournoy in the very early days of his drilling company in Alice.

"He kept them safe, and the rigs were always clean. My dad was one of his first roughnecks—Bill Etheridge, from Dumas, Texas. He went to Rockport to do some shrimping and then that wasn't working out too well so he later hired on with Mr. Flournoy. I was just two or three years old. We lived in San Diego, Texas—not far from Alice—in a duplex apartment when I was a little girl. Mr. Flournoy and Maxine were on one side of the duplex and we were on the other. I was the only kid in the outfit. Another guy lived there who worked for Mr. Flournoy. My dad worked for him from 1947 to 1948, until he got sick. Dad quit working in 1965 and died a year later."

Flournoy also had a knack for hiring the right people, he had good judgment in that way. He could be very demanding and difficult, but he had redeeming qualities. He had a heart for people, and was often very generous. He sometimes got mad at everybody but he'd swing around. He bragged on his employees too, and many people told some really funny stories.

His longtime office assistant, and close advisor, Sue Murdoch said:

"Sometimes we dreaded talking to him, but still we were very loyal. It was just family. See, people to this day wish it was like it was back when

Flournoy had the Company. He would get mad and hang up on us and I would get to the point that I would hang up on him! He always wanted things his way, but as we know in life, we can't have everything our way."

Murdoch, and many others who knew him well, said Flournoy was about the only big oilman in that area who worked hard to improve the town of Alice— dating back to the 1950s when he started making real money. By the 1980s, he was among the 20 most powerful Texans, according to newspapers and magazines, so his influence was heavy.

"His loyalty, you felt safe there. In 1986, we were all like—OK, are we gonna be here even. He kept a lot of us on, if he wasn't mad at you. I put him in a different class than (other area oilmen). He had compassion, and they didn't. He liked powerful people, but he liked regular people, too … he always had good advisors, though he didn't always take that advice. And he was sometimes reckless with his money. He did reward people amply. You just kinda take him as he comes, like any colorful figure," Murdoch said.

"He would go from office to office and you'd hear him say, in his deep, calm conversational tone: 'now, this is confidential.' And go all the way down saying to each person as he entered their office: 'now, this is confidential.' Whatever a waitress said to him, gossip, was law. He would believe people sometimes over us. He was like a relative through long association … He does do things on a grander style than anybody else. He had rig shows, we'd always have them. The business was run honestly. No crookedness. We did things the right way, no sloppiness. That made everything else easy in life. He ran a good ship," she said.

Woods Matthews worked many years as Flournoy's accountant with an office at Flournoy Production Company. He was from the Rio Grande Valley town of Edinburg, near the Mexican Border and graduated from Edinburg High School, and was a top professional who could have gone anywhere.

"We don't agree most of the time, but I've been with him for 24 years. Mr. Flournoy says 'if you can find a better job, good luck.' I went looking and couldn't find one. So, I came back," Matthews said in a 2001 interview. "He is something of a product of his environment but he is a very unique and unusual person. One of his idiosyncrasies is he can alternate between being brutally blunt in his dealings with people, and he can be totally diplomatic, sensitive and compassionate. He had strong opinions. For example, he would say, 'I won't say I disliked so-and-so. I hated him.'"

Flournoy defined the oil business as central to everything that elevates human beings from elemental poverty to middle class and upper-class status.

"The consumption of (oil and gas) distinguishes our country and other advanced economies, from so-called Third World nations. After all, people throughout the world do not truly reach the middle-class until they have a means of transportation, electricity, and electrical appliances and climate control within their houses," he said. "All those things depend on energy. Despite being so essential, the energy business is often misunderstood, Flournoy said.

"People call it the 'oil and gas industry' though in reality, in the developed world, it is more like 'the natural gas—AND oil industry ... in the U.S., we now produce more natural gas in 2002—expressed in both energy equivalent and dollar value—than we do oil and by the year 2020, it is predicted by experts that natural gas will supply almost twice the amount of energy as oil does now. Almost all new electrical power, generated both in this country and in most industrialized countries, will be supplied by natural gas, in large part due to environmental considerations. Natural gas produces far less pollution," he said.

"There is plenty of natural gas to go around. Back in 1980, many people thought the supply of natural gas would run out. In fact, misguided energy policies back then prohibited the use of natural gas for some important purposes because it was thought to be such a scarce fuel with limited reserves. In reality, there is abundant natural gas in North America. Oil is not king or queen—gas is. Myth number two is that the oil and gas business is low-tech and blue collar. When people talk about high-tech industries, they tend to think of Bill Gates and Microsoft, computer chips, and people who make missiles and planes with advanced electronics," Flournoy said. "For many, the oil and gas business has a blue-collar image—the image of the roughneck. Certainly, those of us who have worked our way up from the rig floor are proud of what we have accomplished. Our industry has many entry-level jobs if people are willing to work hard and learn.

"But let me tell you, this business is very complicated. I have a friend who was the deputy secretary of energy of the United States, who asked scientists at our top nuclear weapons facility in Los Alamos, New Mexico, where the most complicated computer problems known to mankind were and they said the most difficult task for the most advanced computer now in existence is in predicting the weather with certainty. The next most difficult task is sorting through seismic data—the electronic recordings of underground soundwaves—to map the subsurface of the Earth to lead us to oil and gas," he said.

"Every day wells are drilled thousands of feet under the surface trying to find and extract oil and gas using metal tubing and cement manipulated by complicated mechanical devices known as rigs. No human being has ever seen oil and gas in its natural state 10,000 feet underneath the ground, honestly, and we do not even know with certainty how it got there. How difficult is finding oil and gas? Geologists will tell you that the average success ratio for drilling exploratory wells is one out of nine. There is no such thing as a sure thing in this business. It is simply too complicated and high-tech. Another myth is that the free market determines the price of oil. Prices go up and down … some people, many of whom are unfortunately either in the oil business or in government believe that these price fluctuations reflect 'the free market' and so we should accept them as a feature of free market capitalism. In reality, however, oil prices are governed almost entirely by governmental policies of various sorts, mostly by foreign governments."

Flournoy said he was probably destined to enter the oil and gas business because Louisiana and Texas production fueled a great deal of the U.S. war machine in fighting Japan and Germany. It made the difference between defeat and victory.

"Is this because most of the oil and gas in the world is in the United States? Of course not. American governmental policies, including private property and tax preferences, helped our industry grow … more than two-thirds of the world's oil and gas reserves are in the Persian Gulf and Russia. The largest oil company in the Western Hemisphere is not Exxon, as some people may think, but instead is PDV S.A., the Venezuelan National Oil Company. Venezuela has twice the proved oil reserves than what we have in the United States."

In early 2020, Iran discovered a new field with an estimated 50 billion barrels of crude oil—and no telling how much natural gas.

Flournoy said the key to where oil and gas gets discovered is governmental policies—principally its laws—belief in free enterprise, and taxes.

"If all the nations in the world had the same property tax laws, tax laws in general, sanctity of contract, bans on bribes and corruption, and other laws, as does the American government, I am convinced that almost all of our oil and gas would be produced from countries in the Persian Gulf, Russia, Venezuela, Iran, Mexico, and other places where finding fossil fuels is much cheaper than in the U.S. We are blessed to live in a country that has good laws, a good economy, a good educational system generally, and sound property rights—compared to most of the world.

"Once people understand that oil prices are dictated by the decisions of governments, concerning how much drilling there should be, what the levels of taxes there should be on both producers and consumers, and the location of pipelines and ports, it should be readily apparent that governmental policies dictate how much energy should be produced, the countries it will be produced in, how much should be consumed, and the source of energy—be it hydroelectric, nuclear power, coal, gas or oil. People who say there is a free market for energy simply do not know what they are talking about," he said.

"Another myth—Americans are the top dogs in the energy business. Back in the mid-70s, the largest oil and gas companies in the world were American firms but now only two of those Top 20 companies are American and all but four are owned by governments—from the Persian Gulf to Mexico, Venezuela, and Russia. In the early 1970s, wherever people went throughout the world they'd find American geologists and engineers were at the very forefront of the energy business. Two trends pose a further threat to the livelihood of Americans in the oil and gas business: first, young Americans are no longer enrolling in significant numbers in our schools of geology, engineering, and other oil and gas sciences. Second, the U.S. is depriving its citizens of great opportunities to work in many nations in the Persian Gulf, where much of the world's oil and gas supplies are. The oil reserves in Iraq and Iran, representing one out of every five barrels of proved oil reserves in the world, will be developed by people from foreign nations."

Flournoy said it makes no sense for our government to deprive

Americans of the chance to dominate the oil and gas industry in other countries when our competitors will simply take our place with their own people.

"Americans have done a lot to glamorize investment banking, lawyering, medicine, and other professions, and we have done relatively poorly in encouraging and facilitating young people to enter science and engineering, or for that matter to work hard to rise in the blue-collar ranks. Can we expect our country to remain at the top of this industry worldwide unless, as a community, as a state, as a nation, we encourage young people to get the education and job experience needed to keep us at the top of the energy industry game?"

"Myth number (I lost count. Is that five? Let's move on ...)", he said, is that the oil and gas business is a good way to make money.

"Some people have been blessed by the business, certainly that is true of my family. But for every one of us survivors, there are quite a few corpses out there. Do not get me wrong. The oil and gas business is about as fascinating as any business out there. It is challenging. A lot of us like the competition, but no one should think that people in the business are all successes or fat cats," he said. "A study by the National Petroleum Council showed that over a 15-year period of time, the average return on refining was somewhere between five and six percent. During the same period, there average return on investments in government bonds was well above that. Even Savings Bonds did better.

"Capital expenditures needed in this business, whether in the production business or in the service businesses, are enormous. And over a long period of time, you simply do not make money if the amount of money you need to pay to replace your reserves or your rigs or anything else that deteriorates, equals your cash flow. Those capital expenditures eat many people alive. I am not complaining. We are proud to be in the oil and gas business. But people who have invested their money in the business have done so, quite a bit, for the love of it and less for the financial rewards," he said.

CHAPTER 13

THE PIRATES OF PETROLEUM

Iraqi leader Saddam Hussein ordered his country's military, on August 2, 1990, to invade their neighbors—Kuwait—with the primary aim of becoming a leading global petroleum power dominating both the Arab world and the Persian Gulf, where much of the world's oil reserves are concentrated, trying to shift the international balance of power. The United Nations instituted an embargo of Iraq. The Western and Arab nations signed-on as well, and defended Saudi Arabia against Iraq. Russia also cooperated in that effort.

Before that time, it was almost fashionable to say that oil was no longer important, and that it had lost its strategic significance. But a coalition of 33 nations, led by the U.S. in a five-week air war and 100 hours on the ground, forced Iraq out of Kuwait. So, Saddam never took possession of Kuwait's oil and gas. The reality is that even today, in 2019, oil is still central to security, prosperity, and the very nature of civilization—though solar and wind power are making big strides to also provide a lot of energy. In recent years, of the top 20 companies on Forbes 500, seven were oil companies. The late legendary Texas oilman T. Boone Pickens invested heavily in West Texas wind power, and saw it was a good way to provide clean energy, along with solar power, and to therefore begin to reduce the need for foreign oil imports and perhaps help reduce the impact of atmospheric pollution on the Greenhouse Effect— also known today as global warming.

Major price movements can fuel economic growth or drive inflation and kickoff recession. Oil is the only commodity on both the business page, and the front page, of newspapers. It is still a massive generator of wealth for individuals and nations.

Japan attacked Pearl Harbor to protect their flanks as they grabbed for the petroleum resources of the East Indies. Hitler attacked the Soviet Union to get the oil fields at Caucasus—a strategic objective. America's predominance in oil proved a decisive factor in American victory over the Germans and Japanese and by the end of the war, they were basically out of fuel.

The Suez Crisis of 1956 marked the end of the road for the old European powers, and it was as much about oil as anything else. Oil power loomed large in the 1970s. It catapulted peripheral nations into great wealth and influence but Russia—a leading global oil exporter--squandered its tremendous oil earnings in the 1970s and 80s on a massive military build-up. Also, where the U.S. was once the world's greatest petroleum producing country, that's ancient history. Now the U.S. imports account for about 50-percent of consumption but that trend has fluctuated in the past 20 years or so.

"We are the hydrocarbon society. Anthropologists will someday refer to us as 'hydrocarbon man'," Flournoy said in 2002, months before he died. The oil business—in the first few years—provided an industrialized world with a new product called by an invented name: 'kerosene.' This new form of light pushed back the night and extended the working days. At the end of the 19th century, John D. Rockefeller had become the richest man in the United States just from the sale of kerosene.

Another flashpoint occurred about 16 years after the Suez Crisis. The date was October 6, 1973—Yom Kippur, the holiest of Jewish holidays. More than 200 Egyptian jets roared into the sky to nail Israeli military positions on the East Bank of the Suez Canal in the Sinai. While that was happening, Syria launched an attack on Israel's Northern Border. This was the beginning of the 'October War' and it was the fourth and most destructive of the Arab-Israeli wars up to that time.

The military hardware involved in this conflict was supplied mostly by the United States and the Soviet Union, but the most powerful weapon of all was oil, and an embargo that resulted in less overall production and export cutbacks to the U.S. and other countries.

The supply-demand equation of oil was tighter than it had ever been since World War II, and while America's economy relied on Middle East oil, the relationship between the U.S. oil companies and the countries exporting oil, was poor. A crisis of global proportions loomed.

On the front page of the November 8, 1973 edition of the Corpus Christi Caller-Times, an AP story headline read: "President Nixon's top energy advisor says nationwide gasoline rationing probably will be imposed next spring."

The story continued: "John A. Love, director of the Energy Policy Office, emphasized that the White House has not made any decision whether or not to order rationing for the first time since World War II during spring—the start of the vacation-recreation season."

Had it been imposed, rationing meant people would apply to local rationing boards for tickets authorizing the purchase of limited amounts of gasoline, depending on the priority assigned. This was all due to the fact that Arab nations decided to withhold oil to friends of Israel.

"Regardless of what happens in the Middle East," Love said, referring to the Arab nations denying oil to friends of Israel, "I can't help but think that we are going to be in a worse position next year in relation to demand than we were this year, by far." Gas shortages started in the summer of 1972, and many stations closed. People drove a lot less, as a result.

Nixon wanted to order that highway speeds be reduced to 50 miles per hour for government vehicles, and also reduced central heating, and cooling levels in homes and offices, and smaller fuel allocations. Britain, Spain and France were not targets of the Arab embargo—it was aimed primarily at the Netherlands and the U.S. Those friends of Israel.

Before the Arab oil cut-off was announced, Nixon Administration experts predicted a shortfall of between 100,000 and 800,000 barrels a day in the U.S. After the embargo, the U.S. faced a loss of between 2 million and 2.5 million barrels per day, and the nation used about 17.4 million barrels a day. The potential shortage was 3 million barrels a day if the Pentagon was forced to use only U.S. production—since the military received about half its supply, or about 300,000 barrels per day, from foreign sources.

Nixon's secretary of state, Henry Kissinger, urged Israel to withdraw from most of the Arab territory it had occupied since the 1967 war when it captured Egyptian, Syrian, and Jordanian territories. Israeli withdrawal seemed the only way to get the Arabs to resume oil shipments to the U.S.

The Alaska Pipeline, all 800 miles of it, was built in the late 1970s for the purpose of getting more domestic oil and it took four years to build. The pipeline would carry about 2 million barrels per day, or about 8.5 percent of U.S. petroleum consumption at that time. This North Slope oil was discovered in 1968, and held an estimated 30 billion barrels of oil reserves. The pipeline begins in the rugged Keystone Canyon area north of Valdez, the ice-free Gulf of Alaska port where the oil was pumped into tankers bound for West Coast ports.

Oil created a "vast, rarified, bafflingly complicated industry," Flournoy said.

"It was cheap to produce in faraway desert lands and expensive to recover elsewhere, so the arid realms of the Arab sheiks gradually developed political wallop."

The first Middle East oil was discovered in 1908, in Iran, and it was exploited by the Anglo-Iranian Oil Company—forerunner to British Petroleum, and six years later Arab oil was gushing. Even with developments globally, by the mid-1950s Texas still had crude oil reserves estimated by government officials at close to 100 billion barrels. Today, West Texas still holds an ocean of oil in the Permian Basin. One recent discovery there is a field estimated to contain roughly 40 billion barrels.

"The Western Hemisphere produces 66-percent of the world's oil, while the Eastern Hemisphere is credited with 34-percent," according to an Oct. 9, 1955 article in the Corpus Christi Caller-Times. "The world has produced to date more than 84 billion barrels of oil, and remaining underground reserves of nearly 155 billion barrels (according to the 1955 edition of World Petroleum Report.")

According to expert estimates, the world still has about 1.5 trillion barrels of oil left that can be drilled and extracted commercially—about 47 years-worth at current consumption rates. Though with increasing population, even with the assistance of wind and solar power, we humans may only have about 30 years left. The time has come for strong U.S. leadership in this area.

President Dwight Eisenhower invoked, in 1959, an import quota system and companies were told by government to the last barrel how much oil they could bring in. Imports then were 1.3 million barrels per day. At the beginning of the 1960s, an oil glut had developed—overabundance. Large international companies reduced posted prices and taxes paid to producing countries. Those producer nations reacted by forming a self-protective organization we know today as OPEC—Organization of Petroleum Exporting Countries.

"King Faisal of Saudi Arabia, since pushing aside his brother Saud in 1962, had seen many a crisis and felt many a pressure from the Arab-Israeli spinoff. Apparently, he felt he had no choice but to promise, however reluctantly, to make his vast riches an Arab oil weapon," said William L. Ryan, in an article published Nov. 14, 1973, by the Associated Press. OPEC first raised prices and then cut production, and this was fully supported by the Soviet Union— since it would do economic harm to the U.S. The Cold War was in full swing.

In 1973, the world still had a lot of oil in the ground—at that time it was thought to be about a trillion barrels. The Middle East had about half that, and the U.S. had an estimated 43 billion barrels—though it was a lot more than that, as later studies would show. Saudi Arabia had more reserves than the rest of the Persian Gulf put together. The non-communist world in 1950 used about 10 million barrels per day, and 25 years later that rose to 50 million barrels per day. Demand was only going to increase. During this time, power plants across the country were switched from oil and gas, back to coal.

It's no wonder the world is heating up as of 2020, with all the pollution from human activity. This creates a condition known as the Greenhouse Effect— where sun rays heat up the Earth but are blocked by this pollutant particulates from exiting the atmosphere back into space. However, even with the threat of acceleration of global warming from powering industry and human activity on a global scale, the current Trump Administration is in total denial concerning this potentially catastrophic problem and old EPA policies that would protect our environment are being scrapped by Trump—who knows little to nothing about the science of anything, especially if it gets in the way of cold, hard cash—the God of modern man.

Yet, this problem wasn't truly realized by top leaders globally 45 years ago. At that time, the concern was powering the engine of industry, and keeping people either warm in the winter or cool in the summer—keeping them moving from place to place in motorcycles, cars and trucks, airplanes, ships, plowing fields and fighting wars—the massive machinery of wars.

"Much of the blame for this energy shortage is easy to place," said Sherman Hunt, president of the Texas Mid-Continent Oil and Gas Association in a Nov.

9, 1973, AP article. "It belongs to the senators and congressmen from 'have not' states, who have done their best to damage or destroy our domestic petroleum industry with unwise legislation in some cases— inaction in others."

Petroleum engineers, in agreement with President Nixon's stated aims for the nation, hoped that the country could become self-sufficient by 1980—and much of this could come from 'enhanced recovery' methods that would yield tens of millions of barrels from oil fields, and the country had enough coal at that time to significantly reduce the effects of the oil shortage. Still, in the early 1970s, many people in the eastern states huddled in the bitter cold because they had run out of heating oil.

Nixon also ordered an end to the all-night floodlighting of the White House, thermostats were turned down to 68 degrees in the Executive Mansion, and heat and lighting in federal buildings was curtailed as well. Air Force One would fly slower to save fuel, and Nixon asked congress for an authorization to cut government and business hours, adjust air and other transport, license nuclear power plants for 18 months without public hearings, establish year-round Daylight Savings Time, and authorize full use of government petroleum reserves.

"Gotta make a livin' he's a Luzianna man" –Doug Kershaw

Chapter 14

An article in the Shreveport Times from 1965 said, "…since Jim Bowie voted for Texas at the Alamo in 1836, Louisiana has been sending men to Texas to succeed. And conversely, Texas has sent us some good folks … let's take the case of Lucien Flournoy, son of Mrs. Lillie Flournoy of Greenwood, who is now a member of the city council of Alice, Texas, and is one of the most successful drilling contractors in the Gulf Coast area," the article states.

"Despite a busy life operating six drilling rigs and employing 112 people, Flournoy comes back to Caddo Parish frequently. There are two big reasons—one is to visit his mother and the other relatives at Greenwood, and the other is to buy drilling rigs from the Brewster Company in Shreveport— one of the best drilling rig manufacturers in the nation.

"Flournoy was born in Greenwood and graduated from high school there in May 1936, which some may remember was still the Great Depression. He was born in an antebellum house and was a member of a family which had settled here in 1836 and was one of the best-known names in the parish. In the Depression days, those two facts coupled with 15 cents would buy a cup of coffee. Fortunately for the local area, the huge Rodessa Oilfield was discovered during this period and after graduating from high school, Flournoy went to work on drilling rigs in Rodessa. The money he earned roughnecking helped put him through three years at LSU in Baton Rouge where he majored in petroleum engineering. His large family pitched in, too, and he always had student work on campus. But the Depression was tough on people, even if they owned good land.

"Leaving LSU in 1939, he worked in a majority of the oilfields in the U.S. as a roughneck, truck driver, driller, tool-pusher, and then to well logging engineer, drilling engineer, production engineer, and finally reservoir engineer," the article states. "Flournoy went on to work for Arkansas Fuel Oil Company, as a production engineer in Alice, and that was a job most men would be willing to keep for a lifetime.

"But this particular Louisiana man had bigger ideas and he began to translate those ideas into a work-over rig of his own design. Working with a welding shop in Alice, Flournoy put all of his savings into the rig which he called 'Old Bread and Butter.' A year before the new rig was ready for drilling, he married Maxine Edmondson, a native of Joplin, Missouri. In the fall of 1947,

Flournoy's rig went into operation on work-over jobs in the Gulf Coast area and it made money from the start.

"It would not be correct to say that all was clear sailing from that day on, because the oil drilling game is about as risky as they come. But today, Flournoy operates six rigs, three of them purchased here in Shreveport, and in the first 10 months of this year his rigs drilled 1,075,790 feet of hole which may be a record. The firm has drilled a total of 231 wells in that period of time including 151 for Shell Oil Company, and 48 for Humble Oil and Refining Company (Exxon). Eight years ago, he organized Flournoy Production Company, which he owns. It operates and manages 32 oil wells with an average production of 25,000 barrels per month and 25 gas wells with an average monthly production of 240,000,000 cubic feet of gas. The newest and smallest Flournoy enterprise is El Salvador Water Well Drilling Company, which has one rig capable of drilling water wells and which is now busy in Central America. Flournoy says the Central American venture is 'sort of an experiment.' If it does as well as 'Old Bread and Butter' we can expect big things.'"

Lucien and Maxine's three children: Mary Anne, Betty Louise, and Helen Ruth, are all residents of Corpus Christi for many years. Mary Anne was born May 9, 1949, at the old downtown Alice hospital, and worked as a physical therapist having earned a degree from the University of Texas Medical Branch in Galveston;

Betty Louise, or "Boo" was born May 19, 1951, in Falfurrias, Texas. She has a degree in physical education from the University of Texas at Austin and was a teacher at Sam Houston High School in San Antonio;

Helen Ruth was born August 17, 1955, in Alice. She majored in physical education at U.T. Austin. Like their mother, the Flournoy Girls were curiously laconic, self-conscious perhaps, about speaking for this biography covering their parent's lives together—though they did laugh about the many times the Flournoy Family would load up and head to Lake Mathis—about 30 minutes by car from Alice. "We had the (lake house) there, for quite some time," Maxine said. "It was good for the kids. We all had a lot of fun especially during the summertime." The girls—especially Boo and Helen—rolled their eyes remembering how their father was so "hands-on" about safety when they were on a boat in Lake Mathis. He sure knew, from experience, how young kids can have a tendency to be reckless, and wild, and he did not want his girls getting hurt.

Mrs. Jackie Richardson, of the Magnolia Ranch, bordering the King Ranch, said in a 2016 interview that Flournoy was a lot different from any of the other oilmen she ever knew. She and her husband were friends of Mr. and Mrs. Flournoy and their kids for years, and one particular memory stood out. It was the image of this seasoned oilman playing the piano in her ranch home—his rough oilfield hands deftly fingering the keys of the grand piano in a large living room.

"It was so surprising to me. I heard the echo of someone playing classical music on the piano and then walked over and looked in the room and it was Lucien! He could play beautifully, as I heard for myself. Very unusual. He was a remarkable man in many ways," Mrs. Richardson said.

His favorite composers were Claude Debussy and Beethoven, but he could play whatever he studied, and with talent. He loved listening to music of all kinds—whatever caught his fancy—and when he drove me around town in his big Lincoln Navigator, or out to oil rigs to visit friends, he would often play CDs of various types, and I remember him tapping his fingers on the steering wheel as he drove while playing "Take 5" by Dave Brubek, and "The 'In-Crowd'" by the Ramsey Lewis Trio. Flournoy was definitely cool. One might even call him "hip." As a liberal thinker, like his ancestors, he was cool.

Mrs. Richardson's aging memory banks were a little sketchy from the maladies of time. She had a pleasant, reassuring and calm voice—the sound of a woman who'd lived through several dry and harsh decades of South Texas.

"We loved the ranch life. I did, and my husband did. We bordered the northernmost side of King Ranch and had about a two-mile fence there. They were such good neighbors and whenever the fence between us needed work, if cattle got loose, why—before you knew it, even before we knew there was any kind of problem, their ranch workers would be already there on our place saying hello and they had work to do. Before you knew it, the fence was in good shape again, and the cattle were all back where they needed to be. Those were the kinenos, or King's men," she said.

The woman, like so many elderly ladies with refinement and education and class, did not curse aloud. She exuded pleasantries, the old Texas, where a handshake was better and more important to people than any contracts written on paper.

"A handshake still goes a long way in Texas," she said, with a chuckle, but a certainty in her voice, an unshakable quality of certitude common among good folks of the land and the small towns from San Antonio to Corpus Christi and Padre Islanders—people who either had something but left it, or had nothing and sought to find something among the shifting sands and towering sand dunes that seemed like a long row of castle towers in the evening wind, as the ocean labored to bring in the tide and driftwood, and if it was a storm many other items would be left on the shoreline.

She'd seen rough weather, and so had her good friend for part of her long life, Jean Carson, a girl who graduated from Alice High School in 1950, and never really left the area either. Why would anyone leave a kind of paradise? Not that South Texas—Alice, Robstown, Kingsville, and Corpus Christi, was the French Riviera. But there was plenty of work and fun to be had, and movie houses were popular ways to pass the hot summer days— with air-conditioning and cool drinks. Gunslingers were often TV and movie house pulp fiction characters dreamed-up and written by young writers with thick glasses and even thicker skulls. That's entertainment— after working a 12-hour day in the humid, windy South Texas summer sun, taking a cool shower, a nice dinner, and a good piece of film noir on the downtown movie screen.

Chapter 15

THE ADOPTED HOMETOWN

In the 1988 book, "Alice: A Centennial History" by Jean Darby, the author pays tribute to the little community's resiliency—like desert cactus or the coyote, possessing unique and vital skills to flourish when most can't even survive.

"Dedicated to those early pioneers who established a settlement on the South Texas prairie at a railroad junction where the large cattle herds came and who had the determination to (establish and rebuild) a town from the ashes into a thriving city," wrote Ms. Darby.

According to Alice Mayor Octavio Figueroa, in his February 23, 1988 proclamation: "...one hundred years ago, on the 22nd day or August, 1888, Alice was officially recognized with the dedication of the Alice Post Office.

"...at the junction of the Texas Mexican Pacific Railroad and the San Antonio and Aransas Pass Railroad—in Alice—there grew the largest cattle shipping center in the world," Mayor Figueroa wrote. His information is easy to verify. This town was not Dodge City—the mythical radio and TV series kind. Alice was rough, and tough, but people were mostly there to do a very hard and often dangerous job—fooling around in the depths and temperament of Mother Nature with mere human tools recently developed.

"(Alice) has grown to be the hub of the petroleum and ranching industries," the mayor wrote.

Lucien Flournoy knew about as much about Alice, as the years would come to pass, as anybody else—almost. He was out-matched in length of residency by only a scattering of surviving old-timers by the time he finally sold the drilling company and delved into many mysterious and unknown investment projects, but "he had a hand in ever-thang," said Tubby. "There's no telling what all he was involved with while he owned the drilling company, but especially later on, too. See, he was always looking, always curious, always trying to find a good deal of one kind or another. He had the money to play with, but his good business head is what really kept him going through good times and especially those lean times."

CHAPTER 16

HEAVY BOMBER PILOT TRAINING

I wanted to know some of the details of Flournoy's military service. He never spoke much about it, but he'd enlisted as a private and was approved for flight training as an aircrewman engaged in early training to fly Army Air Corps bombers in combat. It took a few months, but finally I received his entire military records file from the military.

Getting Flournoy's military records was time-consuming, but the records-keepers in St. Louis did their best and finally located them—a lot of Army records were burned in an early 1970s fire on the giant facility. In those days long before the internet and personal computers that can store files in many areas for safe-keeping—once a record burned that was it.

He served less than two years active-duty, but had an eventful and productive time as an air crewman, and pilot trainee, in the U.S. Army Air Corps—or Air Force. He'd later expand his role, as an instructor for the Air Corps. Captain Anthony E. Karnes, Assistant Adjutant, wrote September 22, 1943, that Private Lucien Flournoy Jr., serial number 19206259, was "honorably discharged for the convenience of the government," adding, "his character is excellent … efficiency rating as a soldier. Very satisfactory." The only problem was his rheumatoid arthritis, discovered after doctors were treating his broken ankle, an injury during training exercises. Flournoy once told me it happened when he fell while running an obstacle course.

A September 21, 1943 report typed up and signed by a military physician, stated Lucien suffered from arthritis in both ankles and knees, and this problem was first noticed in 1941, while he worked in the oilfields.

Further examination showed "arthritis, chronic, recurrent, of arms and feet."

But one other problem shows in his military record, obtained from the National Archives. Lucien was also, while hospitalized, experiencing "glove-stocking hypesthesia, repressed anxieties, neurotic drives ... hospital diagnosis: Psychoneurosis, hysterical type..." Signed by Lt. L.B. James, U.S. Army Medical Corps, Sept. 18, 1943.

Whatever trauma Lucien had experienced, hadn't influenced the commanding officer, who considered him a first-rate pilot trainee. This would have propelled his rank to lieutenant rapidly.

By Feb. 1943 he was stationed as pilot trainee at Santa Ana Air Base, Santa Ana, California. His enlistment record shows he joined the "Air Forces Enlisted Reserves" on December 15, 1942, in Los Angeles. Home of record was 830 Ducommun Street, Los Angeles. Prior to joining up, he's spent the past three years earning about $50 a week as a petroleum engineer. He was listed as married, and signed up for $10,000 government insurance provided through National Service Life. He had a $27 monthly allotment sent to his wife at the time, July 31, 1043, listed as "Mrs. Evelyn Flournoy—partial support." But his mother is listed as "person to be notified in case of emergency." The record also stated he was educated in eight years of grammar school, and four years high school, with three years and one semester majoring in petroleum engineering at L.S.U. At the time he enlisted, Flournoy stated he'd most recently worked operating formation tests as a petroleum engineer. That was good money, especially in the early 1940s, with the nation recovering from the Depression.

His Armed Forces enlistment physical stated he was a Methodist, had blue eyes and brown hair, five-ten, 165 pounds, with perfect eyesight. A few cavities, filled. Tonsillectomy at age 10, an unlisted illness for two weeks at age 16, but no complications. On the date of his enlistment, Lucien was 23 years and six months old.

Captain Harmon C. Bell, Air Corps Assistant Adjutant, wrote a letter about Lucien on September 21, 1943, at HQ, Santa Ana Army Air Base: "The following named aviation cadet, (pilot), this station, having been eliminated from aviation cadet training are released from appointment as aviation cadets, reverted to grade held prior to such appointment ... will be discharged from the Army of the United States without delay by reason of not meeting the prescribed minimum standards for induction..."

Lucien Flournoy's flight training physical showed his medical record prior to joining the Army Air Corps, or Air Force: "measles, mumps, smallpox, influenza in childhood, fractured left radius, 1924; lower 1/3; good recovery. Tonsillectomy, 1930. Surgical removal, foreign body (needle) left knee, 1928; good recovery." He was slightly color blind, but was listed as "safe for air crew" by the examining doctor. Initially, he passed the flight physical exam with no problem.

He would later be assigned as a physics instructor, due to arthritis limiting him physically, and was transferred for the purpose from Santa Ana Field, to a training command near Reno, Nevada, and served as an instructor at the University of Nevada at Reno.

On May 31, 1943, Lucien suffered a knee injury during training: "Strain, left knee, severe, accidentally incurred, while on a cross-country run near University of Nevada, Reno, Nevada, May 17, 1943. Condition on admission: slight pain and swelling of left knee," stated Captain E. F. Tufts, U.S. Army Medical Corps doctor. He was returned to duty June 5, 1943. During the spring of 1943, Flournoy is listed as also experiencing a bad cold, and a right shoulder injury. All during training, regardless of illness or injury, Flournoy gave full attention and effort to his duties, as stated June 30, 1943, in a report signed by Captain Anthony Karnes, acting commander overseeing his work at University of Nevada: "His character is **excellent**. Efficiency rating as soldier—**excellent**."

In early flight training, in California, he qualified for flight above 30,000 feet, at the 33rd Altitude Training Unit, Santa Ana, Army Air Base. June 25, 1943.

But when the base physician at Santa Ana Army Air Field discovered Flournoy suffered from rheumatoid arthritis, he had to follow War Department rules and order him to be medically discharged. The final physical states the arthritis started causing some trouble "in civilian life,

1941" and was detected in both Flournoy's ankles and both his knees. The arthritis is listed as "chronic, recurrent of arms and feet."

On Sept. 22, 1943, Flournoy was honorably discharged from the Army Air Corps, as a pilot trainee—but he is listed at the rank of private. The discharge certificate was sent to his Greenwood address. A few months later, the Army Air Corps was apparently unaware Flournoy had served and on Jan. 15, 1944.

Major General J.A. Ulio, the adjutant general at Headquarters Army Service Forces, Washington, D.C., stating: "…enlisted Reserve Corps Enlistment Record has been received from Lucien Flournoy, serial number 19206259, who enlisted at Los Angeles, California on 15 Dec. 42. A report of change card has been received showing him to be serving on 30 Jul 43 as a member of HQ, AF, PS, P., Santa Ana, California.

"No record has been found of the receipt of a War Department A.G.O. Form No. 183 … showing call to active duty for this man … by order of the Secretary of War."

(Aviation student. July 12, 1943, flight physical cleared by J.W. James, M.D., captain, Medical Corps.)

His home address in the military records at time of discharge is listed as: Lillie M. Flournoy. The address is "Greenwood, LA, Caddo Parish."

Chapter 17

A Time to Build

Flournoy was, like most everybody in the world, tremendously relieved that the United States and the Allied nations prevailed against the Nazis and we won the Pacific War against the Japanese, but he was also happy to get out of the Army Air Corps and back into the oil business as an engineer. He had quite a bit of experience, even at a young age, because he started while still a teenager and he had colorful experiences that he sometimes liked to detail, and laugh about.

"My first roughneck job was in Arkansas, riding to work, roomed with some firemen, and had all my stuff in a paper bag. One of the firemen pulled out a chew of tobacco, the driller was playing some hillbilly music. I am 17, come from a pretty non-hillbilly family history. This was when the Texas governor, Pappy O'Daniel, played on that. I thought it was wrong to use hillbilly music to become governor of Texas," Flournoy said.

"These men went to third grade, if that far. They'd pronounce things like, 'I kilt it' or 'that last job blowed out.'"

He started to laugh: "One time a guy told me for no reason, 'I'm gonna hit you in the mouth.' I told him I had an Arkansas mother, and it kind of calmed him down. He bought me my first pack of cigarettes, Chesterfields. I said, 'I don't smoke.' He looked down at me hard. I said, 'but I get mighty hot sometimes.'"

As stated earlier but briefly, Laurent Flournoy, a well-known landowner and lapidary—cutter, polisher, and engraver of precious stones and jewelry—was then one of a few Protestant residents in the village of Flornoy. He soon fled to Lyons, France, where he married Gabrielle

Mellin, and after the St. Bartholomew's Day Massacre on August 24, 1572, when thousands of so-called Huguenots—or anti-Catholics—were killed, including Gabrielle's own father, Laurent and his wife fled France for Geneva, Switzerland, to avoid death during the religious persecutions.

More than a century later, some of the Flournoy relatives decided to join many other Europeans in traveling and settling in America— the promising new country just beginning to heal from wounds of the Revolutionary War. Some of Lucien Flournoy's ancestors found Virginia appealing, and others moved on to the unsettled land and mountains of Tennessee. A Flournoy grandfather, Samuel, was born October 4, 1724 in Manakin Town, Virginia. He found good land and built a plantation, married Elizabeth Harris in 1748, and had several children. The official marriage certificate dated April 9, 1748 shows the British influence in America at the time: "Know all men by these Presents that we Samuel Flournoy and Henry Wood are holden and firmly bound unto our Sovereign Lord King George the Second and to His Heirs and Successors in the Sum of fifty pounds Curr't to the payment of w'ch well and truly to be made ... the condition of this obligation is such that if there be no lawful cause to obstruct a marriage intended to be had and solemnized between the above bound Samuel Flournoy and Elizabeth Harris then this obligation to be void else in force."

But almost thirty years later, when he was 51, things had changed. Sam Flournoy enlisted with the American forces in Feb. 1777 for three years of service against Sovereign Lord King George and his Red Coats during the Revolutionary War. He served with First Company, Virginia State Regiment, and earned roughly $10 a month until his discharge in March 1780. He died, age 54, from the trauma and wounds suffered in battle, several months later, on Dec. 12, 1780 at his plantation, named Farmington.

Sam and Elizabeth had 11 children, among them an interesting son named Thomas, born in the 1760s, and who continued running his father's Virginia plantation after his father's death. His mother's date of death is not listed, but she willed her two youngest sons—Thomas and Silas— a large portion of the Flournoy plantation, and land she inherited from her father. Thomas must have foreseen his death in the spring of 1794, for he made out his will in March and died six months later. His will provided for the emancipation of his plantation's slaves—probably an unusual decision in those times, since it wasn't until about 70 years later that President Lincoln signed the Emancipation Proclamation.

Silas, the youngest child, was only 20 when Thomas died, and he inherited the plantation. Silas was only six years old when his father died, and a few years later lost his mother. He married Martha Cannon in 1793, and they had 10 children. He was a prominent landowner, and in 1807 bought 600 acres near the Cumberland River across from The Hermitage, and one of his rural neighbors was future general, and U.S. president, Andrew Jackson.

His first son, Alfred, was born at the Farmington plantation Dec. 3, 1796, and was probably as rebellious and adventurous as Silas in his young days—was only about 16 when he joined up with General Andrew Jackson and about as 3rd Lt. in Capt. W.O. Butler's Company, 44th Infantry, received a severe wound in the leg. He is a brave young man and deserves a (full) lieutenancy in the Army."

Just shy of his 18th birthday, Alfred Flournoy was already a disabled war veteran, and his left leg below the knee had to be sawed off. He would never be hindered much by the loss, as he rode horses regularly, travelled widely, and worked heartily, all the rest of his long life. But it did slow him down initially, for a few months, anyway.

On Christmas Eve, 1814, the British and Americans signed a peace treaty in Ghent, Belgium. The warfare between Great Britain and the United States was officially ended, though the treaty was somehow not observed in the forthcoming "Battle of New Orleans."

General Jackson believed black soldiers would be the decisive factor in defeating the British in New Orleans, so he offered slaves freedom if they enlisted with his troops and were the winners. Quite a few black men joined Jackson for the fighting, but Jackson didn't honor his pledge of freedom after the War of 1812's last battle. The greatly angered blacks.

For the rest of his long and generally happy life, Dr. Flournoy had a wooden leg—his friends called him "Indian leg" because his leg was the same as wooden Indians that decorated the local Caddo Parish trading post near Greenwood. But Alfred preferred to use a cane. His particular favorite, with him at every step for years, was a cane with a handle that concealed a razor sharp, five—inch long stiletto that could be instantly pulled out and thrust at an attacker. He was no easy mark, even disabled and in old age.

Dr. Flournoy Greenwood grave

Polk, who had roomed at a boarding house in Washington, D.C., with Sam Houston as a young Tennessee representative, would go on to be elected the 11th President of the United States and served one term, from 1845 to 1849.

This was after he'd served several terms as a Tennessee congressman—the only president in U.S. history (to the present day) to also serve a speaker of the House. He was also Tennessee governor from 1839 to 1841.

Alfred was a strong supporter of Congressman Polk, also a Democrat, and contributed to his political campaigns. In return, Polk helped him, and his brother, obtain land in North Louisiana.

In addition to the friendship between Polk and Alfred Flournoy, the two men were also close to Gen. Andrew Jackson. Polk was a political protégé, and Alfred looked up to Gen. Jackson as a great soldier who saved his life at the Battle of Pensacola. So, both men were interested in helping

Jackson in politics. Had it not been for Jackson's help, Polk likely wouldn't have been elected president. His nickname was "Young Hickory" due to his close ties to Jackson—nicknamed "Old Hickory."

But Polk was an advisor for Jackson in his successful 1828 bid for the White House, so Jackson didn't forget his loyalty and strong support in Congress. Jackson, the first Democrat, was the seventh President of the United States, and served two terms, from 1829 to 1837. Alfred Flournoy was one of the 178 Jackson electors who would make his presidential win official.

Though many of his friends often urged him to run for public office— and he had the means and the backing to make a good showing in most any local election—Alfred just considered politics a sideline. Also, as he said to friends, he was vocally intolerant of people he politically disagreed with, and didn't hold his tongue—he wasn't inclined to be especially diplomatic.

Business was his livelihood and he focused on it, often traveling and being away from home quite a lot, as seen his wife's letters to him. Martha Flournoy wasn't as interested in worldly wealth as he was, it is clear. But Alfred, who could have made a good living as a physician, was a born businessman. This fact was evident once he settled in on good land. He was also physically strong, and possessed great endurance, and worked like a mule to build up his place, with help from workers—who might be Caddo Indian, Latino, black, or a combination of racial and cultural backgrounds. He also believed in paying a fair wage to any man working for him, and helped with medical care.

He wanted, "plenty of the good things in life," as he told a friend. And he wanted to give his family a comfortable life, as he had experienced in younger years on the plantation.

But on September 13, 1834, Alfred lost his dear wife, and it crushed him emotionally. By this time, he was at home more often than not, so he'd been with Martha in the months prior to her death. His mental state was revealed in a September 30, 1834 letter to Congressman Polk.

"My dear friend, you cannot imagine how desolate I am—I have six little children, and there is not a man perhaps in existence who is less qualified than myself to take charge of such a family. My wife was an excellent manager and had the exclusive charge of my household—I had been a great deal absent from my home and ever on my return I found all to my satisfaction. I am at a loss to know what is best for me to do—the more I reflect, the more gloomy and discontented I feel…"

It is clear in the letters exchanged between the two men that whatever favors Congressman Polk did for Alfred, were returned. He was loyal to his family and friends, and if he made a commitment, or a promise, his word was like a signed contract.

On September 17, 1837, he wrote to Polk: "My Dear Friend, Permit me to congratulate you on again being elevated to the Speaker's Chair—I could not help fearing that the changes of the times have been such that your political enemies would have been gratified by your defeat … Since you left, I have sold my land in Giles and shall start in a few days to explore some region more congenial to the growth of cotton…the Red River country.

"The country is yet entirely new—not filled up by settlers and a man can make his choice of the best…it lies on the west side of Red River and near the head of the great Rafe—the country was purchased from the Caddo Indians— the Texas line approaches within some thirty miles of the River at the point near where I would expect to locate," Alfred wrote.

In the fall of 1837, at age 41, Alfred took a friend with him and they rode on horseback from Tennessee to the area now known as Shreveport, and Greenwood, Louisiana. He returned home after making sure it was excellent cotton land, and a good place to build a home and raise his kids.

When he arrived, the family were no doubt overjoyed to see their dad and brother return, since their mother had died only three years before. Her absence would have been painful for the growing children, though they were well cared for by family and friends in the Pulaski, Tennessee area.

He wanted better land, a new start, to leave the old behind and embrace a new life not just for himself but for the whole family. And he was a man of adventure, and uprooting from his home plantation in Tennessee to a new region far away would be a big trip indeed. But one he was fully capable to undertake and manage.

But he would be leaving many dead relatives behind at the family cemetery on Locust Hill—his father, Silas; sister, Eliza, and her husband, Alfred Harris; another sister, Martha Trotter; his own infant daughter,

Eliza; and his wife, Martha, to whom he'd been married from 1819—when she was 16—until her death in 1834. He would also be leaving many living members of his father's family, for a place where he knew nobody. The only one who he wouldn't be leaving was his younger brother, Silas, who was with him on the idea and looking forward to it.

He had the idea that the brothers would build two large flat-bottomed boats to carry everything they'd need for the trip and far beyond their arrival—so they could set up a camp and start building a permanent house. He reasoned the boats could be successfully launched when the nearby Richland Creek was at flood stage.

"Until about 1840 numerous flat-bottomed boats were built at Pulaski and at various points along Richland Creek and Elk River, by which the tobacco, cotton, hemp, and other products were shipped to market; generally shipped to New Orleans ... these boats floated down with the current, and usually required about six weeks to make the descent; under favorable circumstances it was made in less time, dependent on the stage of the water and the influence of the winds," according to family records.

The two boats had to be large enough for all the equipment, supplies, deck hands and future workers for the new farm, and they'd need a cover for use when it was cold and rainy. About 50 of their employees helped construct the two boats in about a month.

The livestock would have to be moved by land, with cowboys on horseback and wagons carrying freight. This group had to also have tools and material for building a ferry to cross the river where none existed—if necessary. And it was probably necessary at least once. Both groups were supposed to arrive at Shreve's Landing—now the city of Shreveport—about the same time. But that didn't happen. The river carried the boats much faster than the overland travelers and the livestock.

When Alfred and Silas left, they took only two family members—Alfred's sons, Alonzo, 18, and James Silas, not yet eight. The date was December 11, 1837, when the two boats were launched into Richland Creek after heavy rains, with the river rising to near flood stage.

Alfred wrote that the black workers on both flat boats shed tears silently as they all worked to enter the river—a dangerous task requiring complete concentration and arduous effort. He felt the same way, as did his little brother, Silas, and their boys. And so did those left behind, some of whom would follow them overland—hopefully arriving at the rendezvous point on the Red River about the same time. That was the plan, anyway.

Alfred led the way, his emotions just as strong as everyone else's about leaving his old home place behind and all it represented, but he was also all-business in tough situations like they faced getting into the river, and started the journey downstream. What might they face on this long adventure? Who might they encounter—how many friends, or enemies? But he was a seasoned wilderness traveler by that time, not to be rattled or dismayed or distracted.

He'd been a soldier, so he would take on the job of river boat captain, with a wooden peg leg to prove he fit the role.

But he kept in mind the entire trip, through whatever adversity came their way, what he'd written to his wife on one of his many business trips: "The prospect of owning virgin Louisiana land, a thousand or more acres of it, capable of producing cash crops of corn and cotton in super-abundance, (is) indeed an appealing and happy dream."

About 20 miles downstream from Pulaski, the two boats would meet the Elk River, near Elkton, and from there were pulled into Alabama meeting up with the Tennessee River—moving west and then north, many miles away from their intended destination. This must have been disconcerting, as the hours and days passed—no doubt cold winds throughout, uncertain currents, sand bars and rocks near the surface. The nights must have had a special factor of spookiness to them, as the boats slowly drifted along. But Alfred made sure the boats were well supplied with food of various kinds, and there'd be no shortage of fish caught along the way, for certain. They had plenty of warm quilts and blankets, even a couple of buffalo hides, and firearms of the day to protect them against marauders or common thieves.

Finally, the two boats met with the Ohio River, and after a few miles along the southern tip of Illinois to the great Mississippi River. Once they hit the Mississippi, it was like a couple of trucks banging along the bumpy back roads, finally reaching the four-lane highway. They'd travel more than 1,500 miles to reach New Orleans, where Alfred sold the flat boats and gained passage for them all on a steamboat up to the mouth of the Red River, and from there upstream to Shreve's Landing—the locale of modern-day Shreveport, Louisiana. They arrived March 13, 1838, with *no reported losses of lives or important freight.*

Shreveport started as the Shreve Town Company on May 27 1836, a real estate brokerage firm named for settler Henry Miller Shreve. Incorporation as a town was realized three years later, and in 1840 it became the seat of Caddo Parish government. Shreveport was named the capital city of Louisiana during the Civil War, after Union forces captured Baton Rouge.

Somehow, the river sailors and passengers did later meet up with those traveling with horses, cattle and wagons by land, and together they rolled on slowly from the river, to the place they'd name Greenwood—near some springs, later known as Stafford Springs.

"It took the Flournoys just two weeks to make the trip from Shreveport to Greenwood. A wagon road had to be cut all the way through a dense and unbroken forest, and the ground was so boggy, pole roads had to be built in many places," according to historian and writer, F.M. Witherspoon, in a Dec.

11, 1923 Shreveport Journal column. It's likely these explorers cut trees into poles and laid them crosswise for wagon travel—a technique later known in the oilfields as "a corduroy road."

The Caddo Indians lived throughout the area, but white settlers were hard to find at that time. When the Alfred Flournoy expedition arrived, there was only one sign of civilization and commerce—Indian Trader Little John's log store. This was the last place to gear up for a chancy trip into the unknown of Texas territory—just a few miles to the west.

Alfred sized up the Native Americans as friendly, not a threat, but often helpful. The only danger he could see were land speculators that would be coming in, he knew, to fight for the best land they could get for growing cotton, and other profitable crops, raising cattle, horses, families. He used his influence with Congressman Polk to help run the Caddo Parish Land Office, to make sure he had the upper hand early-on, even though—in his letters to Polk, he described himself as merely a "squatter" on the land. Some squatter.

He'd already set up camp, was making plans to build his house, and plant crops.

"Having moved from Tennessee and located myself in this section of the country I take the liberty once again to address you," Flournoy wrote to Polk, in a letter dated April 2, 1838.

"...to solicit your aid in a little matter that I feel somewhat interested in..."

He asked Congressman Polk—Speaker Polk—for an appointment to the position of Office of the Register, when a Land Office was established. And he pushed for that, too, stating that the Caddo land he'd seen in this new area was the best he'd encountered anywhere.

"I feel that I could render a faithful and honorable account to the Government of my acts if I were to get the appointment—I know you stand deservedly high with the President," he wrote. "And your recommendation would have its proper influence with him—I have written to you, because I knew I was writing to an old friend..."

Polk wrote Flournoy back by mid-May 1838, but did not appoint Flournoy to the office he sought, because other forces were already at work to open a Land Office in Donaldsonville, Louisiana. The Caddo Indian lands were surveyed by the U.S. government in 1838, and filed a year later at that office. But Flournoy and his brother were allowed to buy the land they'd already occupied, and soon other settlers came marching in from Tennessee, Georgia, Alabama, and South Carolina, later other areas, no doubt.

"They were pioneers, but not the poor and oppressed looking for a refuge. They were for the most part persons of property who brought their families which included their slaves; they brought household furniture and equipment. It was pioneering deluxe. We hear mention of rosewood pieces in the parlor and pea fowl in the park. The times were interesting...," wrote Alfred Bryson, in an Oct. 1956 paper for the North Louisiana Historical Society.

A month after the Flournoy brothers settled into their new location, Silas wrote a letter to his wife, back in Tennessee. The letter is dated April 11, 1838.

"My dear Elizabeth—Four months from home and have not heard a word from you. It would be hard enough to undergo my present lot if we had communication by letter, but to be cut off from that, it is too hard. I cannot stand it. I try sometimes to dispel my thoughts and get them entirely engaged and wrapped in my business, but it won't do. Like the Mighty Mississippi that separates us, they must have vent.

"Brother Alfred and myself will live a mile apart and our road from one house to the other will be as straight as a line and as level as it can be," he continued. "We intend leaving a grove of trees all the way which will form a beautiful avenue all the way. Our sections (of land) lay broadside it and the road will be on the section line. He will leave the trees on his side and I on mine."

When Lucien commissioned this biography in the summer of 2001, a few of those trees, or their offspring, were giants—still alive after about 170 years—all that remained of the brothers and their dreams. Today, those once peaceful and quiet meadows are disturbed by the relentless sounds of cars and trucks on the nearby interstate highway.

The frustrations and fears Silas felt when he wrote that letter and mailed it would be assuaged only when he made the trip back to Pulaski, Tennessee, and convinced his wife and kids to come back him.

The homes in that area were built with pine logs, usually with six rooms, a hall, and a front gallery. Four rooms downstairs, a hall and two rooms upstairs. In those days the kitchens were, like the "restrooms" were set apart from the main dwelling.

Dr. Alfred Flournoy flourished in this new territory, on his new plantation— all his own. He was to be an organizer of the Greenwood Town Company, and also contracted to build the Shreveport and Vicksburg Railroad from Red River to the Texas Line.

Alfred and Silas succeeded when many others floundered and failed, on their own steam, largely due to financial reserves to back up keen intelligence, charisma, astute political sensibilities—apparently something handed down the line genetically. Lucien Flournoy, the oilman, would use his money and power to support strong Democrats—men of the people— from the 1950s to his death in 2003. Former Texas Gov. Mark White was elected to that office in 1982, and Lucien played a big part in his success unseating a rather dark Republican figure named Bill Clements—also an oilman, or a man with oil interests. This was payback, because in 1979 Clements defeated a good Democrat and friend of Lucien's named Dolph Briscoe.

With Alfred Flournoy's help in fall 1842, Alexandre Mouton won the race for Louisiana governor. Inaugurated Jan. 30, 1843, he was the state's first Democrat in the top office. He served until 1846.

Mouton wrote to Alfred on Jan. 28, 1842, from the town of Natchitoches: "I 'reached this place last evening nearly broken down by fatigue. I have not been off my horse for the last eight weeks, during which time I canvassed the 1st and 2nd congressional districts. It is now too late for me to do much previous to the election, it has therefore been decided by our friends here that an express should be sent to your newspapers with letters and also a large quantity of hand bills which contain my views and opinions."

Though the Flournoys were tough men, aggressive in business dealings, their hospitality was also clear—to friends and often strangers.

Natchitoches attorney, William S. Towmey, wrote in his diary: "June 12, 1841, Saturday. Passed the night at Mr. Watson's, two miles from Shreveport, went next day to Greenwood to church—dined at Dr. Flournoy's with Judge Campbell and Mr. Morse—passed the night there in company with Mr. Crane and General Williamson. Next day rode into Greenwood with Miss Martha Flournoy…"

Alfred and Silas would both be prosperous farmers and ranchers on fertile land with plenty of good water, and a lot of sunshine, though the winters could be rough—hard to ride out. In those early days of medicine, any small illness or injury could kill a person, or an animal. The physically weak were quickly weeded out, for the most part, on the frontier. That left mostly the tough and the smart, to run things. Sometimes also the unscrupulous few who dared to encroach on honest men and their property. Frontier justice was not a cliché, it was a harsh reality and, in those times, sometimes people didn't wait for a sheriff, a marshal, or a judge and jury.

Alfred would witness the inauguration of Congressman Polk, after he won the 1844 presidential race, and he was pleased to see the Democrat take office. He agreed with his four goals, as president: reduction of the tariff, an independent treasury, settlement of the Oregon Boundary question, and acquisition of California. He would wind up being successful in most of his objectives—adding more than a million square miles of land to the growing young nation.

And in 1844, Alfred was a local leader in a proposition submitted to the U.S. Congress calling for the annexation of Texas. He signed the petition, along with 123 other prominent men in Caddo Parish, and it was forwarded to the Committee on Foreign Affairs.

Annexation activists, proponents, knew that in the midst of strong opposition from Mexican leaders, Texas had to be quickly woven into the national fabric or it might become a place for organized foreign insurrection and terrorism.

American leaders began worrying about incipient alliances between the sovereign state of Texas and European countries such as France and Spain.

Alfred's petition was sent to the right man—President Polk. His old friend who was aggressive about expanding American territories. He worked on the annexation question with colleagues and advisors, and on Dec. 29, 1845, Texas joined the Union as the 28th state.

The 1860 Louisiana census lists A. Flournoy, Sr., as a 63-year-old farmer with seven children. His second wife, Martha, who he married before leaving for Shreve's Landing, died at age 33 on Feb. 27, 1848. He had 78 laborers living in houses built on his land. He owned 700 acres of "improved land", worth about $10,000—several million in today's dollars—and 500 acres of "unimproved land." He had six horses, 24 mules, 15 milk cows, 10 oxen, 50 sheep, 100 pigs, and 15 head of cattle. Value of his livestock was $5,000.

"In the drought year of 1860 with cotton production at 60-percent of normal for the parish as a whole, Alfred produced 175 bales—about 400 pounds each—of cotton, and about 3,500 bushels of Indian Corn," according to the census. "His personal property values were shown as $20,000 ..."

But a year later, the Civil War broke out, and it would soon impact lives and fortunes. Alfred was too old for any more combat, and he only had the one good leg, so he stayed out of the battlefields—though it's not known what he was up to during the war. He may have moved to another location, but he did survive the war, and lived a fair number of years more. Finally, on Oct. 18, 1873, Alfred Flournoy, M.D., fell ill with Yellow Fever during an epidemic. He died 11 days later. The doctor's bill was $130.

Alfred's brother, Silas, who named his new home "Pleasant Point" when the brothers settled in for the long term, died in 1844 from some kind of accident during a wolf hunt in an area known as Boggy Bayou.

He was only 29, and left a wife and children. His son, Camp, would serve in the Civil War, and Camp's son Lucien, was the father of the subject of this biography. The Flournoys were the Kennedys of Caddo Parish—well-established, successful, handsome people, with nice homes and manners, educated, and a sense of style.

Future generations, after Alfred and Silas built up their land and community, suffered from hard times—most notably the time of privation in the southern states following the Civil War, and then again during the Great Depression and World War II. These folks had a hard time surviving, having to work hard without benefit of many laborers on site. Many formerly wealthy people, and those from long lines of aristocrats in Louisiana history, were forced to either sell land for survival or find work after the Civil War, and upon onset of the Great Depression.

"Dr. Flournoy's dining table, possessing extension leaves to extend it to 12 full feet, was once used by enemy Yankee soldiers as a feed trough for their horses," according to Branches from the Flournoy Family Tree.

CHAPTER 18

DUTY AND COURAGE

Lucien Flournoy's father was the son of Civil War veteran Camp Flournoy, a soldier of the Confederate States of America—the rebels. He earned his legendary status for one single act of courage that meant a great deal to the men of his army unit. Lucien Flournoy was Camp's grandson— both liberal-minded admirers of President Abraham Lincoln. Though the Flournoys fought honorably for the south—mostly for their land and families—some were glad the Union won and pulled the country back together, but Lucien was proud of what his grandfather, Camp, had done. It wasn't at all about slavery for the Flournoys, dating back to their early days of North America. Flournoy's ancestors in Tennessee would free the black people working on the plantation there, near the town of Pulaski, and made sure each one had a trade so they could survive. That was in Silas Flournoy's will, and the family honored that wish—specifically, and to the letter—many years before Lincoln officially declared slavery over with his Emancipation Proclamation. Yet, the government couldn't handle the mass of black people in the south when it came to providing them all with a trade or education of some type, so they suffered more. And for a long time under the White Man's cruel tyranny.

Camp Flournoy was fighting for land and liberty, just as Mexican revolutionary leader Emiliano Zapata and his guerrillas would do in the early 20th century in order to keep corrupt governmental forces from killing him and the villagers of his town, and stealing their land, something that was happening quite a bit in Mexico—especially by the already wealthy haciendados—large ranchers—who used the Mexican Army in a fascist attempt to steal land away from peasants. Camp Flournoy was fighting for the same purpose--though after the Civil War ended, no carpetbaggers would steal one single acre of that original Flournoy land.

Camp Flournoy

While being captured by Union Army soldiers, Camp thought quickly and somehow managed to wrap their all-important "battle flag" about his body under his clothing and their captors almost went mad trying to find it. But they never did. After the Civil War ended, a few years later, the men serving with Camp held a big party for him in the French Quarter of New Orleans, and the event made a big story in the local newspaper—the New Orleans Times-Picayune. The article first appeared in the Shreveport Times, but was carried by wire service throughout the southern states.

The article was published not long after the end of the Civil War, with bold headlines: "Flag of the Nineteenth Louisiana Regiment."

The article stated: "Several weeks since Capt. James F. Uts, President of the Benevolent Association of Confederate Veterans, received of Major Camp Flournoy this old tattered and worn battle flag of the 19th Louisiana Regiment of Gibson's Brigade. This old relic of days of long ago will be unfurled at each regular meeting of the association, to whom it was presented by Major Flournoy. This standard was presented to the 19th Louisiana Regiment on its reorganization at Corinth, Miss., in May 1862. It passed through the fiery ordeal on many hard-fought fields, including Jackson, Miss., Chickamauga, Missionary Ridge, the Georgia and Tennessee campaigns, under Generals Johnston and Hood, to Spanish Fort, in Mobile Bay, to the surrender of the Confederate Army, which took place at Meridian, Miss., on the 10th of May, 1865. Its last appearance on the battlefield was at Spanish Fort, which was held for several days by about 2,000 men, under Gen. Randell Gibson, now U.S. Senator, against over 20,000 Federal soldiers and several gunboats combined. In that conflict the flag was cut half in two by the explosion of a shell. Major Flournoy, at the surrender, took this flag from its staff and substituted in its stead the company flag of Robin Grays of Fillmore, Bossier Parish, which was better known as the Butler Flag, taking its name from the gallant and beloved first captain of that company, London Butler, who, as Major commanding the 19th, was killed like his sire, the Colonel of the Palmetto Regiment in the Mexican War, at the head of his regiment while making a charge. Major London Butler was killed at Chickamauga.

The Yankee major whom the 19th Louisiana Regiment surrendered raised objections in receiving the Butler Flag, claiming it was not the battle flag of the regiment. Major Flournoy, however, evaded this dilemma, and finally succeeded in bringing the flag of the regiment concealed in his shirt. It had been loaned to the Benevolent Association of Confederate Veterans, and, as we have said, will be unfurled at each regular meeting of the association."

According to Flournoy archives, "the dozen or so years immediately following the war were years of change, and all Southern aristocracy found the transition difficult and hard. The Flournoys and their kin were not exceptions. Some, especially planters and landowners, never learned to cope successfully with their changed circumstances. Often, no doubt, in the midst of the heat and toil and sweat of their daily struggle for existence, they dreamed of better days … of the wild rides after the fox and the deer; of the lolling, the nap on the balcony, in the summer house, or on the rustic seat on the lawn; of the long, leisurely meals, the after-dinner cigar; of the polished groups in the easy but vivacious conversation in the parlor; of the chivalrous devotion to beautiful women; of pleasant evening drives; of visits around the plantation, with its long, broad expanse of waving green, dotted here and there with industrious slaves; of the long rows of negro cabins with little picaninnies playing about them; of the old well and its beam and of the women with pails of water on their heads; of the wild old field airs ringing out from the cabins at night …"

"My mother's father, and her mother, were born in Mississippi and after my mother's father died, they all went with their widowed mother to southeastern Arkansas on an ox cart," Flournoy said. "During the Civil War, Grandfather Gabriel, or Gabe, buried his meat when he heard some of the Union soldiers were coming. He was at home when the soldiers arrived on his place. They uncovered all of his meat and used it to supply the troops. Then, they came back and took his beloved Stetson hat off his head, and rode away."

Chapter 19

RAINBOW LUCK

When I spoke more by telephone with former Gov. Bill White, he noted that Flournoy knew more about South Texas politics—and the 20th century history of it—than anyone else he knew.

"I don't know anybody else who knew George Parr—the famous or infamous Duke of Duval County, as he was dubbed by some newspaper reporter long years ago—AND Gov. John Connolly. He knew that crowd. Gee whiz, the guy spanned a very different world, and he had the foresight to pave the way for the next couple of generations of politicians. I can't think of anyone like him now in Texas politics," White said.

"He was kind of a 'king of the hill' of the old, older, but also was not afraid of change. Many people like to keep things the way they are. I had grown up in San Antonio, and my involvement in politics began on the West Side. When I was very young, my dad coached baseball in the 1960s on the West Side," he said. White said that in the area where he grew up, the Church was involved in the civil rights movement, and families were involved in the Church, and this would help Latino leaders get into state offices.

"We made a lot of progress from the time the Voting Rights Act of 1964 was signed by President Lyndon Johnson, to the time I ran for governor—in 1982—in registering people to vote, especially in the minority communities. When I ran, it was only 18 years after the poll tax was abolished, where minority citizens had to pay if they wanted to vote," he said.

"I met Lucien and he asked what we could do to make South Texas more powerful politically. I started doing some research. Though the poll tax was long gone, we Democrats still did not have the turnout needed to create a constituency that would effect political change. Lucien went to work, and he went county-to-county. There are a lot of successful people who may be able to call a governor or a lieutenant governor, but not too many people who know who all the county commissioners and constables are. Very few people know them. He knows them," White said, in the 2002 interview. "As a result, we had a higher turnout in the primary than in the general election."

Flournoy realized fully that South Texas would only prosper when people there started voting a lot more, so he organized a widespread *get out the vote*. "He understood the big picture, and he understood South Texas, and over time people began to see clearly that South Texas could be a swing vote and it was a swing vote," he said.

White served one term during a terrible time in the Texas oilfields—the mid-1980s--when the price of oil dropped precipitously. He called a summer 1986 special session of the Texas legislature to address the economic urgency of diversifying the economy and not rely so much on the oil and gas industry. A lot easier to say, than to implement on a broad scale.

"The end of the oil boom was in 1982, the tail end of it and the bust was just beginning. Two places were being drilled a lot—South Texas and the West Texas Permian Basin. The number one producing area, in the number one producing region, on planet Earth during the 60 years he's been in the business," White said.

By the time we arrived in Alice, in June 2001, Flournoy—at age 82--was starting to suffer quite a lot from skin cancer, prostate problems, emphysema, and heart trouble—mostly angina pectoris, which is pain caused by coronary artery blockage. This condition is normally managed well by nitroglycerin tablets placed under the tongue, where the medication dissolves rapidly and enters the bloodstream. This was almost instant, welcome relief to Flournoy.

But his doctor visits for health conditions kept him away from the office a lot, during that year.

I had plenty of time to go around town and speak with friends, former workers, colleagues, and people who benefitted from Flournoy's generosity over a period of decades, and I found out he a friend of the Parr family, based out of San Diego, Texas—a dusty little town a few miles west of Alice. He'd drilled wells on Parr property, and got to know George Parr and his nephew Archer Parr, both loyal Texas Democrats like Flournoy.

Parr was vilified in the right-wing media, especially, for his money and political power among Texas Democrats—at a time when Texas was mostly a rural state and the people had more common sense. Texas was run by Democrats, like Congressman and House Speaker Jim Wright, and future U.S. president, Lyndon B. Johnson—both political powerhouses.

Chapter 20

Skies of Fire

(Back in 1954 the town of Alice held an oil show and published a program entitled "Blowout", a copy of which was made available to us by a man in Freer. Published in this program were a number of stories then told by old timers about blow-outs which had occurred during their lives. We reprint them here as examples of some of the experiences of the oil fields of (the old days)

SEELIGON

"The worst blowout that I recall in the Seeligson Field was on the Magnolia No. 7 A.A. Seeligson in August 1937. I was there when it happened, probably because we drilled into the soft sand too fast and our mud was light. It blew out and we caught fire about 12 days later and burned for 10 or 12 days. First, we got our equipment off, then we had to take trucks and lines to saw the casing in two. The thing was blowing straight up and welders went in with shields, under streams of water till they got right under the blaze, where there was a draft and it was fairly cool. They welded the big casing to the little casing, and then we could cap it," said Earl J. (Big Boy) Stanley, of Falfurrias, in an interview years ago.

JIM HOGG

"It happened in 1926 down in the Thompsonville Field in Jim Hogg County. Those were the good old days of wooden derricks, steam rigs and tailored cement sack shirts. We expected trouble. We were running pipe trying to keep the hole full of mud and hoping she wouldn't blow. The driller put his foot on the fly wheel to kick it off center when suddenly there was a terrible banging and a horrible scream. I was lucky. I flew to the brush. Looking back, I saw the driller lying stretched out with his leg caught in the fly wheel, flopping his arms and yelling 'cut the steam.' The derrickman and toolpusher were in the slush pit. My roughneck partner landed on his face from a guywire contact. The fireman died nicely. You know, a loud yell and a hammer banged on a drill pipe can cause a man's guts to get blown out," said Alonzo H. Curtis, of Pearsall.

PALACIOS

"I have seen quite a few blowouts while working with the Texas Railroad Commission on the Lower and Upper Gulf Coast, and just between us they are all the worst. One of the worst I ever saw was the Sun Oil Company Number 1 Bayshore Farms wildcat near Palacios, Matagorda, County in January 1938. It happened when the drill pipe was being pulled out of the hole with the testing tool after the completion of a drill steam test around 10,000 feet. The well had been kicking and two additional blowout preventers had been installed. Two Halliburton trucks also were on the scene to compound their pumps so that the kicking could be overcome. In minutes the derrick and rig were a mass of flames with an estimated 8,000 barrels of oil burning per day. The equipment was molten metal in a short time," G.P. Colinos, of Beaumont.

NUMBER 7 RACHAL

"I used to hear some of the old-timers argue about whether the No. 7 Rachal, which blew out in January 1928, had as big a fire as the old well that blew out in White Point back in 1915 of 1916. I don't know about the old one but I can guarantee you the one I saw was a booger," said S.W. Blount, Jr., of San Antonio. "The No. 7 Rachal was drilled by the late John Bartlett and other partners in the old Saxet Company, who were the first men to successfully find a market for, and deliver, the gas that had been known to exist at White Point at least since 1904," Blount said.

"(The well) bottomed-out at 2,312 feet, the No. 7 had been producing gas for a line that ran to Corpus Christi. One day it broke out and started making mud water and gas from outside the surface casing about 15 to 20 feet from the well. The crater enlarged, snaking its way until it got to the well head. The Christmas Tree and casing weaved a little while and then broke off and fell into the crater. Al the pipe and fittings fell, the well ignited," according to "Historic Legends of Western Oil" compiled by Fred Cook, and published for oil and gas professionals years ago. The long-defunct magazine was provided for this book by Jean Carson, of the Coastal Bend Geological Society.

The magazine story titled "Blowout!" states: "Some sequels to this blowout, which was reported to have been seen as far away as San Antonio are as follows: an Englishman was sitting in the Nueces Hotel Lobby and heard some oilmen discussing the blowout. When he heard one say, *'and when the Christmas Tree fell over, the fire started.'* The listener interrupted the oilmen to ask: *'I say, were the candles lighted (when the Christmas Tree fell)?'*"

The San Antonio Express, with the dateline of Corpus Christi, reported: "The burning gasser (well) has become a natural glass factory. Particles of a translucent, glass-like substance are being erupted heavenward, volcano-like, and falling to Earth again on the crater's rim."

According to the magazine, Tex Thornton was the famous oil and gas well fire blowout specialist called to the scene of No. 7 Rachal (location). First, he dropped a 25-pound charge of nitro into the flaming crater and when that didn't work, he followed up a couple of days later, with a 50-pound charge that extinguished the blaze "in a matter of seconds."

In connection with No. 7 Rachal: a car came rattling over the rough streets of Corpus Christi and a woman stepped out and asked how to get to the fire.

Advised by a policeman to stay away, she then told them she was Mrs. Tex Thornton and had driven all night to bring him a load of nitro. Directions were hastily drawn-up, and the streets even more quickly emptied, according to the magazine.

In an explosion heard for many miles, a second well was attempted in 1913 at White's Point. This well reached 2,195 feet (deep) before it blew out. The (blast) was heard for miles and it is estimated that over 60 million cubic feet of gas daily was destroyed. The crater is said to still (be visible), according to the magazine.

One gas well fire in the Corpus Christi area burned for almost 10 years before it could be effectively extinguished by blowout specialists. Those years of spewing gas completely wasted an entire gas field. The crater was all glass, caused from the intense heat liquifying sand.

R.B. BRYANT NO. 2

"This well was properly called the East Alice Operators Committee and R.B. Bryant No. 2 on the Ingram Farm. The old W.R. Davis Cycling Plant then was under construction," according to the magazine. "This was the second such plant ever built (the first was the Corpus Christi plant in the Stratton Field). The plant was to take gas from the old Tom Graham and Alice fields and a distillate well just outside the plant fence had been completed and shut in awaiting completion of the plant.

"Apparently, a casing leak developed in the distillate well, charging water sands. One of the water wells which got the treatment was an 850-footer (depth) in the plant yard and naturally its geyser was higher than the others. An Otis Pressure Control crew came in and drilled a directional well to control the blowout, and things finally quieted down. Meanwhile, the traffic had to be detoured for 70 days as U.S. Highway 281 was covered with gooey mud. The completion of the Davis Plant was delayed about three months," the story states.

"The cleanup was rough. It cost $35,000 just to get the mud out of the plant yard. No telling what the rest of the cleanup cost. In most places the mud couldn't be bulldozed off. Pumps were set up and the mud was broken down with water before it could be moved," wrote J.T. Traywick, of Alice.

Of course, no petroleum products at all could move anywhere without the Valero Refinery, among a few smaller ones, in Corpus Christi. Officially known as the Bill Greehey Refineries just north of downtown Corpus Christi, these are two refineries—East and West as they are known. The first refinery facility was built in the early 1980s—the West Plant. The second one was built in 2001—the East Plant. Together, these two plants can process almost 400,000 barrels per day. This crude, after it is refined into gasoline, provides much of the gasoline used in Corpus Christi, San Antonio, Austin, and the DFW area, Flournoy said.

Drilling and locating oil and gas is up to the independent oilman or oil-person, or corporate drilling company, and pipelines carry what comes from these wells on to the refinery, to cut transportation costs significantly, allowing for a lot more profitability. And the refinery has the means for wide distribution, and that's good for sales. The other production aspect, beyond an oilman's control, is OPEC and global politics. Whether a legislator is a Republican or Democrat doesn't matter to an oil and gas well driller/producer, as long as he or she supports policies that enable and demand stable U.S. production.

While Flournoy was highly intelligent, especially in mathematics and physics, and did very well in those two subjects at L.S.U. for three full years, he deferred to, and greatly admired, oilfield geologists. He owed a lot of his success to geologists he said many times. Men like his good buddy, Tubby, and others like Jon Spradley—from Shreveport, Louisiana.

"Following my discharge from the army, I took a summer job in Corpus Christi with Jones & Laughlin Oil Field Supply. My work sometimes consisted of delivering equipment to well sites. During those deliveries, I think my interest in geology was first aroused by the fact that the only men wearing clean clothes and sitting in air-conditioned trailers were the Company Geologists `sitting the wells'. South Texas summer temperatures convinced me the air-conditioned trailers were the place to be," Spradley stated.

"After several discussions with my boss, a retired Kansas school teacher, I was convinced that a geology degree was a great way to be in the oil business.

After a search, it appeared four colleges offered geology which concentrated on the oil business. Not necessarily in order of merit they were: LSU, Texas A&M, University of Texas at Austin, and Oklahoma University. I chose LSU because my father's Shreveport address afforded me the opportunity to take advantage of LSU's $30 per semester tuition available to state residents. (Not a bad deal for a person on $110/month G. I. Bill.)," he said.

"At LSU, I was able to double-up on geology courses, having had all of my basic courses and electives behind me due to three previous years in college.

In the three years at LSU, I graduated with a B.S. in Strat/Paleo.

"After turning down an offer from Pan American Petroleum (AMACO) to be a Micro-paleontologist in their Houston Lab, I decided to stay at LSU and get a Master's Degree. I was awarded a teaching assistant-ship and graduated in two years with an M.S.," Spradley wrote.

"The M. S. brought a new offer from Pan American Petroleum for a whopping $25.00 per month more than their offer two years earlier. However, with the new offer was the opportunity to become a 'full-fledged" Geologist in their Corpus Christi District Office. I accepted the offer.

"During my three years at Pan American, I met a number of independent geologists who were able to work when and where they wanted – not bound by structured office hours or limited assigned areas of exploration," he stated. "Independency seemed like the thing for me – but I realized that an intermediate step would be necessary to really learn more of what an independent should expect from this business.

"With that in mind, I down-sized from Pan American and accepted a "two or three-year position (lasting 15 years) with Jake L. Hamon, an independent oil operator in Dallas. My primary reason for the extended stay with Hamon was the 'override' I earned or production found in the Corpus Christi District. We drilled many wells and enjoyed a great deal of success. (Hard to leave a job like that!) In 1978, Jake Hamon became ill and virtually inactive, so I formed Spradley Energy, Inc. and became a full independent. During my stay with Hamon, another reason for becoming a geologist became apparent to me. I fully and finally realized I was working among a select group of fine scientists whose primary strength was their basic honesty toward geology and what the E-logs dictated," he said.

"In our quest for the '*giant Easter egg*', we *all* try to construct the most correct map possible and sometimes our prospects 'drill out' and sometimes they don't – but we have tried our best. We have all drilled 'dry holes', but we can still revel in the fact (that) U. S. Independents are responsible for 80percent of domestic discoveries," Spradley said.

"By the way, a side light and one of the highlights of my 50 years of showing *deals* to many great geologists, it was always the opportunity to present a prospect to the person I consider the geologists' geologist, Joe McCullough.

After the '*showing*' I always came out of Joe's office knowing more about my prospect than I knew before I went in.

"If you ever have the opportunity to show your South Texas prospect to Joe, you will be happy with how much it can help you down the road. And finally, as I move deeper into my autumn years, I continue to realize that subsurface is the real fun in the geology game, especially when it all falls into place and your prospect drills out as mapped. Keep shuffling those logs and the prospect will usually appear," he said.

"Try to always remember that a discovery can make you a wealthy man – not only in money, but also in the knowledge that you have proven to yourself that you are an oil finder."

The Chisholm Trail runs through just about the center of Texas as an old cattle trail for sprawling herds of beef headed from South Texas to a big payday at the railroad in Kansas. A fork of that trail became what is now a four-lane highway known as Interstate 35. The Trail was a big boost to Texas for several reasons—economic and reputation-wise. Texas cowboys, due to the tremendous amount of cattle herding activities, became legendary worldwide. Later, movies only enhanced this reputation situation—though the truth is that real life in the Old West was quite a lot different from the way it's often depicted in TV shows and movies. Cowboys didn't always carry a revolver, and these young workers were taught discipline through harsh conditions, and they'd just as soon avoid trouble as find it. So, shoot-outs were definitely not tolerated by any responsible and respected trail boss—or the head man of a cattle herd. There are always bad people, and good, in any generation.

Texas came to be famous for cattle, and much later crude oil. This attracted people with knowledge and skills in those areas. Like geologists—essential for any independent oilman such as Flournoy.

"In life, some things come from vision and planning. Other good things come from hard work. Discovering my passion for geology came from sheer dumb luck," said former South Texas geologist Duncan Chisholm.

"I should have discovered geology sooner. It was in my blood — literally. My great-grandfather, John Chisholm, died prospecting for gold out west. My father, grandfather, and three uncles all spent their careers in the mining industry. Dad even majored in geology. I was exposed to mining and geology through such glamorous summer jobs as laying new railroad track into a limestone quarry and manually loading limestone blocks onto trucks," Chisholm said. "I now suspect that my father helped me get these jobs not to encourage an interest in geology, but to motivate me to get a college education so that I would not have to do such backbreaking work as a career.

"What did I decide to major in when I got to college with all of that mining exposure? Why, Spanish, of course. I had just spent a year in Bogotá, Colombia as a high school foreign exchange student, was fluent in Spanish, and absolutely loved the South American people and cultures. Of course, I had no idea what I was going to do with a Spanish major, but it seemed logical at the time," he stated.

"The course of my life changed dramatically with what I thought was a simple decision. Dartmouth is a liberal arts school, and I needed one more course to fulfill my science distributive requirement. I had put off taking that last science course, and it was now fall term of my junior year. I made the relatively random decision to take the introductory geology class, and the rest, as they say, is history. I could not believe how incredibly interesting the class was! I was totally hooked. Even though I was just a couple of courses away from finishing my Spanish major, I decided I had to change my major to geology. That change made my junior and senior years pretty intense, but my new-found passion for geology made it all worthwhile," Chisholm said.

"The last part of my story is how I became a petroleum geologist. I immediately went on to Stanford after graduating from Dartmouth. I decided to go into mining like the rest of my family, and Stanford had a very good mining geology program. I discovered, however, that I did not have that same passion for my new geology coursework and decided it was due to a lack of enough real-world working experience to which I could apply the knowledge. I took a leave of absence from Stanford after two terms and was hired by Getty Oil for six months to hike deserts, climb mountains, and look for gold, silver, and copper. It was an extremely exotic experience, but I ultimately realized that I did not have a passion for mining geology. There did not seem to be any reason to return to Stanford to finish my master's degree, and I found myself with no plans for the future for the first time in my life," he said.

"Here is where the second stroke of dumb luck came to the rescue. I had been based in Salt Lake City with Getty. Once my job was over, I spontaneously decided to go back to Stanford one last time to see my friends in the Geology Department, and I delayed heading back home to Ohio where I would have to ultimately figure out what I wanted to do with my life. My unannounced arrival on campus ended up being on the first day of a two-day geology job fair. That evening there was a reception with the recruiters. All my friends were going to be there, and the college provided free food and booze! I did not think that it could get any better than that until I met two really terrific Sun Oil geologists. The next thing I knew, I was in Dallas with a four-month job exploring oil and gas for Sun. After mapping for only a couple of weeks, I was amazed that anything could be so interesting, challenging, and fun. I had rediscovered my passion for geology. I immediately went back to Stanford, and in nine months, finished my master's degree in petroleum geology. I am fortunate to be able to say that the challenge and creativity involved with oil and gas exploration has kept my passion for geology alive throughout my career," Chisholm stated.

Chapter 21

THE KEY-WEST CONNECTION

Had fate or something like it failed to intervene at one point when Flournoy was having hard times in the oil drilling business—a gloomy time for independent drillers—he would have been out-of-business, said his longtime buddy and colleague, Linnie Key, who lived a few blocks away from Flournoy's office in a big, nice, new brick home in the nicest neighborhood in Alice. And Flournoy returned the favor several times over as the years passed.

"I was doing some scouting for the Birdwell Oil Company, and met Lou—went to his office. He was an engineer then, and I rented office space from him. He did a good job. He was all-business, treated people fair. We used to drink coffee together at a café, the Palace Grill on Hwy. 281 when it passed through town. It was owned by Gus Touchmeller—I believe that was how he spelled his last name. All the oil people and towns people in general, would go there in the mornings," Key said.

"I was a land man, leased properties, checked titles, contracts. Back then, dry holes used to be prevalent" before technology made drilling for crude more accurate and lucrative, Key said.

"Lou was all business. He liked to talk about his business and rigs and was really proud of his safety innovations in the oilfields. To save his men. He had 335 people on payroll with hospitalization," Key said.

"I learned structural engineering, taught there at Naval Air Station Corpus Christi, and became acquainted with Lucien late in 1949, and we became friends a few years later. When the company I worked for transferred me to Alice, we became close friends. He was an aggressive and honest person. He talked a lot, and had a lot of interesting, and good, ideas. He was humorous, and enjoyable to be around," Key said. "Then, I wanted him for a customer, and he was hurting there for a while. I would later open Linnie R. Key consulting.

"I started out as a roughneck. He was needling me to come down to Alice and work for him. In 1969 I said give me 30 days. July 1969, I came down to Alice. Assistant to the president. He was a great drilling supervisor but needed me with the business side. He could not bring himself to walking up and saying 'you are not doing the job.' He just wasn't like that. He always remembered how he felt coming up the hard way. He knew how brutal the work was to those guys out there on the rigs.

"I kind of did that (fired people). I told him I would work one year, and this went on for four or five years. At the time I was around retirement age. But he wouldn't let me quit, really, and I didn't really want to anyway. Lucien was just very, very aggressive. One time he walked into Red's office. We also built offshore production platforms. We would build substructure ourselves. Flournoy said let's do the hand-shake. Red, Pete, and Jimmy. We named the rig "Key-West". It was our drill idea.

"If you had a better idea than him, he'd welcome it. The trucking department (was) always one of his pet peeves. He was always making sure everything was working or being fixed with the trucks, and they were absolutely vital to our operations," Key said. "He designed a 'rig in a rush' and other things. He would sit around thinking, drawing little pictures and planning things."

For example, Key said, Flournoy designed all his Weevil Pins four inches high, to carry spare tires behind the truck cab, to make it easier (fixing a flat).

"He was constantly drawing up and dreaming up," he said.

"Accidents were terrible. For one of his men to get hurt it just really hurt him. His rigs, his men, his business, were all part of him. But he empathized with the men because he'd definitely been there and knew what it was. One time I said, 'you're gonna have to lay off'--he would just look at me or something else and whistle a little and change the subject," Key said.

"After my first wife died, Lou's wife Maxine was so worried about the people I was associating with she came up with somebody for me to meet.

She introduced me to a woman named Liota, and it was the best thing that ever happened…," he said.

"Another feature about him, he enjoys people. Gets a big kick out of entertaining. He's an extrovert. We'd never do anything underhanded, it's just our personal lives were pretty reckless."

Flournoy was in dire financial straits at one point when the oil business was hurting in South Texas and elsewhere, due to too much oil on the market and a variety of other factors.

"I said to him, don't get mad. It's very difficult not to express (anger). We got out of those scrapes, had been in two or three of those. But I told old Wilson (a colleague), he'll make our company millions. Flournoy was just tough. You could get him down and stomp on him but he's still gonna get back up and whip you."

Key said he knew a banker in East Texas that might lend Flournoy enough money to drill another well, and Flournoy couldn't get a loan from South Texas banks, probably because all the money for oilfield speculations had already bent loaned out. But Key's friend in East Texas wanted to meet Flournoy so they drove to the little town and met the banker and took him out to eat and had a few drinks and Flournoy's personality won him over. He agreed to loan him the money and he did. That saved Flournoy's business, Key said, and he never forgot that favor.

"He never reneged on any kind of payment. He'd give his last dime to pay back wherever it was he owed. I got my nose in his books. I told him what it all meant. I told him, this is what you make and this is what you owe. We got the debts all at one place. We paid off all the loans at one time. He said, well I believe we can handle this," Key said.

"There are always good times, and bad times, and you can prepare but sometimes you just can't predict. A bad period was 1971-72. Tough time for the oilfields. A lot of time off or "TOs". OPEC countries like Saudi Arabia, Venezuela, etc. Oil was being produced at such a rate it was more than the world needed. So, the independents like Flournoy were hit hard. But things began to bloom again later when he made a big discovery."

Key was born in Tennessee and went to East Texas at age 12. Graduated high school in 1935, had two scholarships.

"I went to what is now Lamar. I got a job in Houston for H.K. Ferguson. I talked my way into the job, $3 a day five times a week--$18 a week. I told my company to send me to Corpus Christi. Went there for a week and sent a wire that said I quit. Without having another job," he said. "I fiddled around down there. I joined the Navy and was in for three years. After the first year in the Navy I learned as much as I needed to know. After the end of the Navy, I went into the dump truck business. Then Wilson Supply business. W.D. Wilson. Formed new division in Alice. We had dances and parties, cotillion clubs. Partying get togethers, BBQs, where Flournoy Park is now southwest of town. In the forests of Mesquite trees. In those times, nothing was really planned, it just happened."

Flournoy indirectly paid Linnie Key back by using his heavy connections to get a new hospital build in Alice. The old one was way out of date. The new hospital was modern and up-to-date, especially for emergencies like car wrecks and heart attacks.

"I had a heart attack a couple of years ago, and the hospital doctor gave me a shot that cost $4,700. A clot buster. Yes. It saved my life though," he said.

"One of the notable Alice independent drilling company owners was a man named Hank Harkins. Hank didn't like Lucien. He was a good manager, but a terrible personnel person. They were competitors, rivals and there were personal reasons, too. Hank always wanted to outshine Lucien. I was president of Alice Aviation. Hank hangered his plane in our (Flournoy) hangar.

Lucien wanted his own plane. He'd been leasing them. We bought a brand- new twin turboprop. He was paying out $20,000 a month on that. And it was a million-dollar plane. The people who worked for me, Flournoy had to learn how to manipulate. It was part of his system. He had to think smart, and he had to pick good people, good operators, because bad decisions like that are very hard to get over. That's why he got the Exxon contract to drill a thousand wells in and around King Ranch."

Thousandth Well

Though he sometimes let himself run a little wild, Flournoy had amazing powers of concentration, and boundless energy for most of his adult life.

"He just walked away from cigarettes," Key said. "The booze was a different matter. He had to get some help with that. Like most people do who dip their beaks too deep in the bottle. You know, it's like when you're younger, you can have a few no-strings flings before you get married … but if you get married to booze, you get divorced from life."

CHAPTER 22

REVERBERATIONS

Flournoy: "Tony and I have never enjoyed each other. That's kind of like saying, we don't give a damn about each other. Also, I was at a store downtown, and I talked to your lovely wife, who I like better than you," he said right to my face, without smiling. He started whistling again—and I think I did too. Flournoy could get you uptight if he was in that kind of mood. You had to take it lightly, not too seriously, as Sue told me several times after he'd chew me out. She could hear it clear up in the front office even with his door shut. Having done very well in military boot camp years earlier, Flournoy's angry challenges were not a particular problem. But getting detailed information—and keeping him on a train of thought—were persistent difficulties for me in the writing of his life story. He rambled, and that made it hard to write in a linear fashion—so I said to hell with it. Just write the story.

"A girl in Greenwood named Geraldine Gooding was my first love. Letters to her were the only ones I'd ever sent. She dropped me a letter once. Then she dropped me, too," he said, with a smirk as he reached to the front of his spartan desk and pointed to a framed business card Flournoy got from President Harry Truman. He also got calls in his office from President Jimmy Carter, when he was president, to big oilmen all over the world. Not counting the countless political powerhouse people, he knew closely and confidentially.

"Four women really meant something to me," he continued, as he swiveled the chair back and forth slowly. "My mother, Geraldine Gooding, my first wife, and Maxine."

As we sat in silence for a few minutes, I kept scribbling and he kept whistling, then decided to talk about another matter: "I was talking to Mark White about running for governor. We ran Mark White for governor and he won. I drew a line on the map and it was South Texas. I explained to him, that's how we got you elected governor. The Hispanic vote. And in 1976, the groundwork we did for Jimmy Carter. We had Texas for him. The groundwork we did set it up.

Controlling Flournoy in a conversation was as useless as trying to corral a wild horse. Jump on him and let him take you for a bareback ride. A real ride through the vast plains of his memory. Wild winds and lightning and him looking intensely as he surveyed the horizon. That's where he sweated blood as a young man, planned on and made his fortune in the decades ahead.

"I helped elect Gov. Dolph Briscoe, too. It was a good thing his daddy made all the money for him, because he couldn't have. He was easy to confuse. And he hired people to get drunk for him, he had so much money, and land," Flournoy said, chuckling.

"I never really had much interest in those playboys born with the golden oil derrick in their baby crib," he said. "People don't realize nowadays but like at LSU, I remember one kid standing ahead of me at the telegraph office on campus said he had only a certain amount of money so he had to make the message short, he told the clerk. So, he finally shortened it to: "To Dad. No Mon. No Fun. Your Son." And a while later that kid came up to our room and he had the return telegram from his dad and it read: "To Son. Too Bad. So Sad. Your Dad."

CHAPTER 23

TOWN ON THE MOVE

Alice grew due to the oil and gas drilling business beginning in the early 1970s—then it was mostly crude oil—and the population expanded from 10,000 residents to about 30,000 in only a decade, said Jim Wells County Commissioner Lawrence Cornelius, a longtime Flournoy friend.

"The County Commission here approves the budget for all the county agents, the roads. I enjoy it. It's O.K. We used to use caliche on all the county roads, it was cheaper and more plentiful than anything else, but now most of the traveled roads are well-paved, pretty well kept maintained," he said, explaining the very basics of his elected position.

Cornelius went on: "He's probably the most benevolent man in the area. Very few people of his status that were as concerned for the well-being of others …

He has a lot of interests, very politically connected. He usually supports Democrats, but I don't think he likes to leave anyone out. I think he learned his politics from business… I don't mean the corrupt part of it, but the functioning of (politics)," Cornelius said.

"I had a cousin was a county commissioner and died July of last year. Flournoy and the Bradfords (brothers who owned a large Alice car dealership) they asked me to run. I won the election, was the first Republican elected in Jim Wells County in a long time. Flournoy said to me, 'Lawrence, you are the first Republican I have ever voted for' and he laughed and shook my hand. He didn't take himself too seriously even though he usually had a serious look on his face and worked constantly."

Cornelius worked as a younger man building houses, churches and schools, and in the mid-1950s moved into oilfield work, and pipelines.

"I did some work for Flournoy, Union Pacific, Arco, Mobil, Pennsylvania United Gas of South Texas, Southern Minerals, Sun Oil. A lot of those either merged or moved out over the years," Cornelius said, relaxed behind the big desk in his Courthouse office in downtown Alice.

"Because Alice was so good to him over the years, he made sure to put his money back into the city," he said. "He takes a stand, but he is not real vocal about it. Like the water bond that passed to repair and renovate public works. He was very instrumental behind the scenes. Repair and renovate water lines in town, and connecting these to Lake Alice—just outside town."

"Flournoy was key in the Alice Industrial Foundation. He was also very instrumental in keeping Halliburton here. Exxon and Mobil used to be here. It takes some influence and reputation to be able to keep (companies interested) otherwise you don't get to talk to the players, the company leaders. It works only if you can get on the inside track. Just keeping the companies here in Alice has been a real economic boon. A lot of companies like his, that size, could have relocated to Houston. But lucky for us, Flournoy was committed to Alice. He was a Louisiana boy, and he was proud of that, too."

Chapter 24

TIME PASSENGERS

Thinking about the very interesting, and determined, man that Flournoy would become, knowing as much about who he really was? It had taken time and patience. He was not so humble as he was just kind-hearted and smart and rangy as an old mule. Brute mental strength—and a tough farm boy raised to have good manners when out of his family's earshot. Beneath a kind smile was that golden heart.

"I served a career in the FBI, and Flournoy and I had been friends for years," Agent Raul Salinas said. "He crossed the railroad tracks to help a lot of people. A very kind person. Cared a great deal for his employees. He never really got the big recognition he deserved but he was VERY powerful and a solid person. He also had a lot of humor in him. We had some good times.

"Lou IS still a legend, years after his death. The other thing I forgot to tell you Is how many people he helped out of poverty. Or helped get medical attention.

He never publicized it. And Dr. Hector P. Garcia really liked him, and he liked Dr. Garcia of Corpus Christi for his selfless work helping the poor and sick," Salinas said.

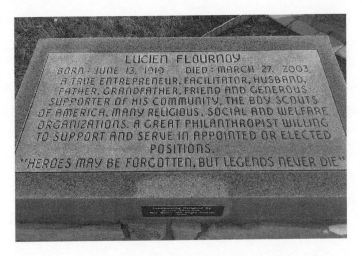

LUCIEN FLOURNOY
BORN : JUNE 13, 1919   DIED : MARCH 27, 2003
A TRUE ENTREPRENEUR, FACILITATOR, HUSBAND,
FATHER, GRANDFATHER, FRIEND AND GENEROUS
SUPPORTER OF HIS COMMUNITY, THE BOY SCOUTS
OF AMERICA, MANY RELIGIOUS, SOCIAL AND WELFARE
ORGANIZATIONS. A GREAT PHILANTHROPIST WILLING
TO SUPPORT AND SERVE IN APPOINTED OR ELECTED
POSITIONS.
"HEROES MAY BE FORGOTTEN, BUT LEGENDS NEVER DIE"

Lou's Last Words

But there was something that preyed on Flournoy from time-to-time. Like so many good men heralding the world with a dying but still living honesty and a gleam of joy in their faces as they try to stride the world.

The great early 20th century American novelist F. Scott Fitgerald didn't realize it a century ago in one of his great novels but he covered Mr.

Flournoy so well, in Lucien's final moments there in that small Corpus Christi hospital overlooking the bay, and far across, on a distant dock, marking it with a haunting green light, a faraway beacon—a light I had dreamed on and laid my own hopes upon at times. Darkened by the Bay shadows—my life still chugging, thinking, finding new roads. *One day long in the distance.*

He was often thinking of his first wife—and cared for her in her mental illness that made him get psychiatric care for her in their 20s. He made sure she was well looked after in her institutionalized state. He had not seen her in many years. This beautiful blond who loved him in her arctic desolation.

"And as I sat there brooding on the old, unknown world ... I thought of Gatsby's wonder when he first picked out the green light at the end of Daisy's dock. He had come a long way to this blue lawn, and his dream must have seemed so close that he could hardly fail to grasp it," Fitzgerald wrote. "He did not know that it was already behind him, somewhere back in that vast obscurity beyond the city, where the dark fields of the republic roll on under the night …"

Mr. Flournoy began to breathe slower, more laboriously, early on the morning of March 27, and later I felt that some spirit had led me there, among the small, quiet, South Texas oilfield townspeople. I could see that fine, courtly gentleman there standing, waving back to a very distant and strange final morning--after a lifetime of spirited adventure. He was truly a friend to all mankind—for the betterment of all.

THE END

Drill Bit

Juan "Chuy" Hinojosa

John Flores truly captures the strong and distinctive personality of Lucien Flournoy, the legendary and self-made oilman and philanthropist known to many as "Mr. South Texas." Lucien is brought to life through the fascinating accounts of his journey to success that brought tremendous benefits to South Texas.

An entrepreneur who was as quick with a political contribution as he was with a joke, Lucien took risks and reaped the benefits of his keen business skills. He gave generously to local, state, and national Democrats and his oilfield inventions made him not only wealthy but powerful politically. Often sought as an advisor by numerous elected officials from the courthouse to the White House, Lucien consistently used his influence for the betterment of South Texas.

It is an honor to have called Lucien my friend and constituent. An honest and good man, he never ceased to give of himself. His extraordinary story is creatively shared with us in John's biography as Lucien Flournoy embodies a true servant leader.

He touched the lives of thousands of South Texans through his giving of invaluable time, money, and influence as well as his public service as Mayor of the City of Alice, that stimulated economic growth and improved the quality of life for not only Alice residents but all South Texans. Because of his commitment, we have countless projects and programs maintained today in the areas of higher education, healthcare, highway infrastructure and many others.

With John, we honor and thank Lucien Flournoy for his selfless contributions to his community and to his friends. He will long be remembered for his kindness and generosity and his sincere devotion to his family, his employees, and his beloved South Texas.

Juan "Chuy" Hinojosa
Texas State Senator, District 20

Capitol 3E.10 · P.O. Box 12068 · Austin, Texas 78711

Juan "Chuy" Hinojosa

Boone Pickens

260 Preston Commons West
8117 Preston Road
Dallas, TX 75225

October 31, 2018

Mr. John Flores
2901 Christine St. NE
Albuquerque NM 87112

Dear John:

Thank you for your letter, and inviting me to participate in your book project. As requested, here are a few sentences on the independent oil man.

"The independent oilman in Texas has always been cut from a different cloth.

Over a lifetime in business I've had to make a lot of tough calls – right and wrong, and many of them very public. Good calls have made me a lot of money, and I've lost my ass on the bad ones.

Fortunately, I've been right more often than I've been wrong.

Oil people in America have been its ultimate entrepreneurs. They are independent, driven risk-takers who have fueled the growth of the robust American economy for generations.

They provide the fuel that drives our engines and factories and the building block for products that touch every part of our lives. And the challenges and rewards in the business are greater today than ever — this is one of the most exciting times to be a part of the energy sector."

Good luck with the book. Please send me a signed copy when it is published.

Sincerely,

Boone

T. Boone Pickens

jer

Courtesy photo

Lucien Flournoy loads drums for his newly founded oil company in 1948. Flournoy, now 80, grew up in poverty in Louisiana. He has done almost every job on an oil rig.

Courtesy photo

Lucien Flournoy with a drilling rig he designed and built in 1947. The rig, called Old Faithful, was the foundation of one of the largest independent drilling companies in the nation, Flournoy Drilling Co., which made him a multimillionaire.

BIBLIOGRAPHY

1. *Wooden Rigs—Iron Men*, by Bill and Marjorie Walraven.
2. *Alice: A Centennial History, by* Jean Darby.
3. *A Primer of Oilwell Drilling, Seventh Edition*, U.T. Austin.
4. *Young Bussey—Young Stud*, by Ralph B. Cushman.
5. *History of Louisiana: From its First Discovery to the Present Time* C. Bunner.
6. *Historic Legends of Western Oil, Volume IV*, Fred S. Cook.
7. *City of the Mardi Gras*, by Harry DeVore, Jr.
8. *Branches of the Flournoy Family Tree*, by Wayne Spiller.
9. *The Life and Legend of Leadbelly*, Charles K. Wolfe.
10. *The Great Gatsby*, by F. Scott Fitzgerald.
11. *How to Like People*, By Robert Jackson.
12. *Personal Notes from Interviews.*
13. *Newspaper archives nationally and Texas/Louisiana.*

John W. Flores has three books published to date. He was born in Dallas, Texas, served four years active-duty as a search-and-rescue crewman in the U.S. Coast Guard, and attended University of Texas at Austin where he studied stage acting and playwriting. His play, "The Five Dollar Bottle" received great reviews from his visiting professor, the legendary Dr. Ted Shine, of Prairie View A & M. As a career journalist, a lot of the work investigative, Flores received several awards. Marine Corps Commanding General James Conway awarded the U.S. Navy Meritorious Public Service medal to Flores via the 4th Recon Battalion HQ for his years of research and writing that have illuminated courageous leaders in the Marine Corps and the Navy.

Glossary

abandon *v*: to cease producing oil and gas from a well when it becomes unprofitable; to cease further work on a newly drilled well when it proves to contain unprofitable or no quantities of oil or gas. Also abandoning, abandonment.

accelerometer *n*: a device that reacts to changes in acceleration used in directional drilling as a way to determine the angle of the borehole with respect to vertical. As the hole takes on an off-vertical angle, the speedometer detects the subtle change in the acceleration of gravity that will be proportional to the hole angle.

acid fracture *v*: to part or open fractures in limestone formations and reach pathways along the fractures using hydrochloric (HCl) acid under high pressure. See: *formation fracturing.*

acidize *v*: to treat limestone or other formations with the appropriate acid for the purpose of increasing the rock permeability near the wellbore.

aft *n*: back of a ship.

air drilling *n*: a method of rotary drilling that uses compressed air as the circulation medium. Natural gas can be substituted for air.

air hoist *n*: a hoist operated by compressed air; a pneumatic hoist. Air hoists are often mounted on the rig floor and are used to lift joints of pipe and other heavy equipment.

alternating current (AC) *n*: electric current that reverses direction. The opposite of direct current (DC) which always flows in the same direction. AC current is widely used in power generation because it is more economical to transmit.

American Petroleum Institute (API) *n*: oil trade organization (founded in 1930) that is the leading standard-setting organization for all types of oilfield equipment. It maintains departments of production, transportation, refining, and marketing in Washington, D.C. It offers publications regarding standards, recommended practices, and bulletins. **www.api.org**
anchor point *n*: a drilling line securing device that is fastened to a derrick or substructure leg. The anchor point must be strong enough to support the load carried by the deadline. See *deadline anchor.*

angle of inclination *n*: in directional drilling, the angle at which a well diverts from vertical; expressed in degrees, with vertical being (I).

annular blowout preventer n: large valve, usually installed above the ram preventers, that forms a seal in the annular space between the pipe and the wellhole or, if no pipe is present, in the wellhole itself. The seal is formed by a flexible element that is hydraulically forced to take on the shape of whatever is in the bore of the preventer, Compare *ram blowout preventer.*

annulus *n*: the space between two concentric circles. In the petroleum industry, it is usually the space surrounding a pipe in the wellbore, or the space between tubing and casing, or the space between drill pipe and the wellbore.

anticlinal traps *n pl*: hydrocarbon structural traps closed in by an anticline or arch, anticline *n*: rock layers folded in the shape of an arch. Anticlines sometimes trap oil and gas.

area drilling superintendent n: an employee of a drilling contractor whose job is to coordinate and oversee the contractor's drilling projects in a particular region or area. The drilling superintendent usually has responsibility for several drilling rigs.

artificial lift *n*: the use if artificial means to improve the flow of fluids from a production well.

assistant driller *n:* a member of a drilling rig crew whose job is to aid and assist the driller during rig operations. This person controls the drilling operation at certain times, keeps records, handles technical details, and, in general, keeps track of all phases of the operation. See *driller.*

assistant rig superintendent *n:* an employee of a drilling contractor whose job includes aiding the rig superintendent. The assistant rig superintendent may take over for the rig superintendent during nighttime hours. The assistant rig superintendent is sometimes called the night toolpusher. See *rig superintendent, toolpusher.*

automatic cathead *n*: spool-shaped attachment on the catshaft. An automatic cathead is located on both sides of the drawworks on the catshaft. The driller can activate the cathead by pulling a control lever on the drawworks control panel. Automatic catheads are used to pull a chain up or break out joints of pipe. See *breakout cathead, friction, cathead, makeup cathead.*

automatic pipe racker *n*: a device used on a drilling rig to automatically remove or insert stem components and store them temporarily in the fingerhead of the derrick. It replaces the need for a person to be in the derrick or mast when tripping pipe into or out of the hole.

B

background gas *n*: a small, measurable volume of natural gas carried in the drilling mud as the well is being drilled. The gas is not necessarily from any of the sediment layer and is not considered an indicator of a commercial accumulation of natural gas. It has a base line value against which any changes in the natural gas content of the mud can be compared.

back off *v*: to unscrew one threaded piece (such as a section of pipe) from another.

back up *v:* to hold one section of an object such as a pipe stationary while another section is being screwed into or out of it.

backup tongs *n*: a wrench that is placed on the drill string below the joint being added or removed. The wrench is secured to a derrick leg to prevent the drill string below the joint from turning.

bail *n*: curved steel rod on top of the swivel that resembles the handle, or bail, of an ordinary bucket, but is much larger. The bail suspends the swivel from the hook on the traveling block. The two steel links that suspend the elevator from the hook are also called bails. *v:* to recover by lowering a cylindrical vessel called a bailer to the bottom of the well, filling it, and retrieving it.

barge *n*: flat-decked, shallow-draft vessel usually towed by a boat. A complete drilling rig may be assembled on a barge and the vessel used for drilling wells in lakes and inland waters and marshes.

barite *n*: barium sulfate, BaSO4; a dense mineral frequently used to increase the weight or density of drilling mud.

barrel (bbl) *n*: a measure of volume for petroleum products in the United States. One barrel is the equivalent of 42 U.S. gallons or 0.15899 cubic meters. One cubic meter is equivalent to 6.3 barrels.

bed *n:* a specific layer of earth or rock that presents a contrast to other layers of different material lying above, below, or adjacent to it.

bedrock *n*: solid rock just beneath the soil.

belt *n*: flexible band or cord connecting and wrapping around each of two or more pulleys to transmit power or impart motion.

bent housing *n*: the bottom portion of a drilling motor, near the bit, that can be adjusted to a small angle. The use of a motor with a bend in the housing allows the well to be steered in a predetermined direction.

bent sub *n*: a short cylindrical device installed in the drill stern between the bottommost drill collar and a downhole motor. It deflects the downhole motor off vertical to drill a directional hole. Bent subs have been largely replaced by bent housing motors.

BHA *abbr. bottomhole assembly*

BHL *abbr. bottomhole location* bit *n*: the cutting or boring tool used in drilling oil and gas wells. The bit consists of cutters and circulating ports or nozzles. The cutters can be steel teeth, tungsten, carbine buttons, industrial diamonds, or polycrystalline diamond compacts (PDCs). Bits can be a roller cone style where three cones hold the cutters and roll on the bottom of the hole on bearings. Or, a bit can be a drag style where there are no moving parts and the cutters are dragged across the face of the rock by the motion of the drill string or downhole motor.

bit cutter *n*: the teeth or cutting structure of the bit.

bit sub *n*: a sub inserted between the drill collar and the bit. See *sub*.

blind ram *n*: an integral part of a blowout preventer that serves as the closing element on an open hole. Its ends do not fit around the drill pipe but seal against each other and shut off the space below completely. See *ram* and *shear ram*.

blind ram preventer *n*: blowout preventer in which blind rams are the closing elements. See *blind ram*.

block *n*: one or more pulleys, or sheaves, mounted to rotate on a common axis. The crown block is an assembly of sheaves mounted on axles at the top of the derrick or mast. The drilling line is strung over the sheaves of the traveling block, which is raised and lowered in the derrick or mast by the drilling line.

blooie line *n*: a large diameter pipe used in air or gas drilling that conducts the air or gas returns flowing out of the well to a safe location away from the rig.

blowout *n*: an uncontrolled flow of gas, oil, or other well fluids into the atmosphere or into an underground formation. A blowout, or gusher, can occur when formation pressure exceeds the pressures applied to it by the column of drilling fluid.

blowout preventer (BOP) *n*: one of several valves installed at the wellhead to prevent the escape of fluids either in the annular space between the casing and the drill pipe or in open hole (i.e. hole with no drill pipe) during drilling or completion operations. See *annular blowout preventer, ram blowout preventer*.

BOP Stack *n*: the assembly of blowout preventers installed on a well.

bore *n*: the inside diameter of a pipe or a drilled hole. *v*: to penetrate or pierce with a rotary tool.

bottomhole *n*: the lowest or deepest part of the well. *adj*. pertaining to the bottom of the wellbore.

bottomhole assemble (BHA) *n*: the portion of the drilling assembly below the drill pipe. It can be very simple—composed of only the bit and drill collars—or it can be very complex and made up of several drilling tools.

bottomhole location (BHL) *n*: the location of the bottom of a well that has been deviated from vertical.

bottomhole pressure *n*: the pressure at the bottom of a borehole caused by the hydrostatic pressure of the wellbore fluid and, sometimes, by any back-pressure held at the surface, as when the well is shut in with blowout preventers. The bottomhole pressure may also refer to the pressure contained in the reservoir.

bottom plug *n*: a cement plug that precedes a cement slurry being pumped down the casing. The plug wipes drilling mud off the walls of the casing and prevents it from contaminating the cement. See *cementing*.

box-on-box *adj.* a type of rig substructure using steel frame boxes to elevate the rig floor.

brake *n*: a device for arresting the motion of a mechanism, usually by means of friction, as in the drawworks brake.

bread-and-butter *n*: Flournoy's first hand-made drilling rig made from his own blueprints. This rig type was highly popular mostly due to dramatically reduced drilling time.

break out *v*: to unscrew one section of pipe from another section, especially drill pipe when it is being withdrawn from the wellbore.

breakout tongs *n pl*: tongs that are used to start unscrewing one section of pipe from another section, especially drill pipe coming out of the hole. See *tongs*.

break tour *v*: to begin operating 24 hours a day.

brine *n*: solution of salt and fresh water.

British Thermal Unit (Btu) *n*: a measure of the energy content of a substance. One Btu is defined as the amount of heat necessary to raise the temperature of one pound of fresh water one-degree Fahrenheit. For example, the energy content of natural gas is often found to be around 1,000 Btu per standard cubic foot.

bulk tank *n*: on a drilling rig, a large metal bin that usually hold a large amount of a certain mud additive, such as barite, that is used in large quantities in the makeup of the drilling fluid.

bullwheel *n*: one of several large wheels joined by an axle and used to hold the drilling line on a cable tool rig.

C

cable-tool drilling *n*: a drilling method in which the hole is drilled by dropping a sharply pointed percussion bit to the bottom. The bit is attached to a cable, and the cable is repeatedly raised and dropped as the hole is created.

cable-tool rig *n*: a drilling rig that uses wire-rope cable to suspend a weighted chisel-shaped bit in the hole. Machinery on the rig repeatedly lifts and drops the cable and bit. Each time the bit strikes the bottom of the hole, it crushes rock and "drills" deeper. Rotary drilling rigs have replaced cable-tool rigs.

cap *n*: to control a well that is flowing out of control; often accomplished by attaching a valve in the open position on top of the well and then closing it to seal off the flow.

cased *adj.* pertaining to a wellbore in which casing has been run and cemented See *casing*.

casing *n*: steel pipe placed in an oil or gas well to prevent the well hole from caving in and, if cemented in place, to prevent movement of fluids from one formation to another.

casing crew *n*: the employees of a company that specialized in preparing and running casing into a well. The casing crew usually makes up the casing as it is lowered into the well. The regular drilling crew assists the casing crew.

cathead *n*: a spool-shaped attachment on the catshaft. An automatic and friction cathead are located on both sides of the drawworks on the catshaft. Catheads are used to pull a rope or a chain to hoist objects or for use in making up or breaking out joints of pipe. See *automatic cathead, breakout cathead, friction cathead, makeup cathead.*

catwalk *n*: a platform on the side of the drilling rip used as a staging area for tools, pipe, and other drilling equipment.

caving *n*: collapsing of the walls of the wellbore. Also called *caving in*.

cellar *n*: pit dug in the ground and lined with either concrete, wood, or corrugated metal, that provides additional room between the rig floor and the first element of the wellhead to accommodate the installation of the blowout preventers. This allows for the used of a wide variety of wellhead types without altering the height of the substructure.

cement *n*: a powder consisting of alumina, silica, lime, and other substances that hardens when mixed with water. Extensively used in the oil industry to bond casing to the walls of the wellbore and to seal unwanted portions of a well.

choke manifold *n*: an arrangement of piping and special valves, called chokes. In drilling, reservoir fluids and drilling mud are circulated through a choke manifold when the blowout preventers are closed. This allows the well to be kept under control.

Christmas tree *n*: the control valves, pressure gauges, and chokes assembled at the top of a well to control the flow of oil and has after the well has been drilled and completed.

circulate *v*: to flow from a beginning point in a system and return to the starting point. For example, drilling fluid is pumped out of the suction pit, down the drill string, out the bit, up the annulus, and back to the pits while drilling proceeds. This process is called circulating drilling fluid.

compound *n*: a mechanism used to transmit power from the engines to the pump, the drawworks, and other machinery on a drilling rig. It is composed of clutches, chains, and sprockets, and a number of shafts, both driven and driving. *v*: to connect two or more power-producing devices, such as engines, to run driven equipment, such as the drawworks.

condition mud *v*: a process whereby the drilling mud properties are adjusted to desired levels. It is done by circulating the mud through the mud system and adding whatever chemicals and liquids are necessary to adjust the properties of the mud.

conductor hole *n*: the starting hole for the well. It contains the large diameter conductor casing that prevents the hole from caving in and conveys or conducts the drilling fluid back to the mud system while drilling the next section.

confirmation well *n*: the second producer in a new field, following the discovery well. A confirmation well is placed at a strategic location designed to prove or disprove the size of the reservoir. There may be more than one confirmation well.

connection *n*: the action of adding a joint of pipe to the drill stem as drilling progresses. Or a section of pipe/fitting to join pipe-to-pipe or to a vessel.

contract *n*: a written agreement that can be enforced by law and that lists the terms under which the acts required are to be performed. A drilling contract covers such factors as the cost of drilling the well (whether turnkey, by the foot, or by the day), the distribution of expenses between operator and contractor, and the type of equipment to be used. *v:* to decrease in size.

core *n*: a cylindrical sample taken from a formation for geological analysis. v: to obtain a solid, cylindrical formation sample for analysis. See *sidewall core, whole core.*

core barrel *n*: a tubular device. For whole cores, it is usually from 10 to 60 feet long (three to 18 meters) and is run at the bottom of the drill pipe with a core bit or head and is used to store and recover the core sample that is cut. For sidewall cores, the barrel is an empty tube about two inches by three inches and is fired into the side of the hole from a sidewall core gun. The sidewall core becomes lodges in the short barrel and is retrieved from the well.

crane *n:* a machine for raising, lowering, and revolving heavy pieces of equipment, especially on offshore rigs and platforms.

crane operator *n*: a person responsible for the use of the cranes on a rig. A member of the support crew on an offshore rig.

crew *n*: the workers on a drilling rig, including the driller, the derrickhand, and the floorhands. Also called *crewmember*.

crown *n*: the crown block or top of a derrick or mast.

crown block *n*: an assembly of sheaves mounted on axles at the top of the derrick or mast and over which the drilling line is strung. See *block*.

crude oil *n*: unrefined liquid petroleum. It ranges in density from very light to very heavy and in color from yellow to black, and it may have a paraffin, asphalt, or mixed base.

cuttings *n pl*: the fragments of rock broken by the bit and brought to the surface in the drilling fluid.

D

Darcy *n*: the measure of permeability (square meters), named after the French engineer Henry Darcy.

daywork contract *n*: a type of drilling contract where the work performed under the contract is paid for by a certain amount each day.

DC *abbr: direct current.*

deadline *n*: the drilling line from the crown block sheave to the anchor that does not move.

density log *n*: a device used to measure the porosity of a formation. The device measures the response of a formation when it is bombarded with gamma rays. The response is proportional to the bulk density of the formation. The bulk density is made up of the amount of rock and fluid present in the formation. Therefore, the log is a measurement of the formation porosity if the type of rock and pore fluid are known. The gamma ray source and the detectors are mounted on a pad that must be placed in contact with the borehole wall. Due to the requirements that the pad be in contact with the wall of the hole, the density log is not used inside of casing.

derrick *n*: a large, load-bearing structure usually of bolted construction. In drilling, the standard derrick has four legs standing at the corners of the substructure and reaching to the crown block. Compare *mast*.

derrickman *n*: the crewmember who works on the derrick "monkeyboard" and handles the upper end of the drill string as it is being hoisted out of or lowered into the hole. This person is also responsible for the circulating machinery and the conditioning of the drilling fluid.

development well *n*: an exploitation well drilled in proven territory to complete a pattern of production.

diamond bit *n*: a drill bit that has small industrial diamonds embedded in the matrix or bit face. Cutting is done by the rotation of the hard diamonds over the rock surface being drilled.

diesel engine *n*: a high-compression, internal combustion engine used extensively for powering drilling rigs. In a diesel engine, air is drawn into the cylinders and compressed to very high pressures; ignition occurs as fuel is injected into the compressed and heated air. Combustion takes place within the cylinder above the piston, and expansion of the combustion products imparts power to the piston and other mechanics working the machine.

direct current (DC) *n*: an electric current that moves only in one direction. DC current is often used to power the traction motors on an electric drilling rig. Compare *alternating current*.

directional hole/drilling *n*: Intentional angular drilling. Deviating from vertical to reach underground reservoirs.

doghouse *n*: a small enclosure on the rig floor used as an office for the driller and as a storehouse for small equipment.

downhole *adj., adv*: pertaining to a location in the wellbore.

downhole blowout *n*: an unintended and uncontrolled flow of fluids from one reservoir to another, never reaching the surface. Definitely avoided if possible.

downhole motor *n*: a drilling tool made up of a helical rotor and stator in the drill string directly above the bit. This motor causes the bit to turn. The rotor turns when drilling mud is pumped through the motor.

Drake well *n*: the first well drilled in the United States in search of oil. Some 69 feet (21 meters) deep, it was drilled near Titusville, Pennsylvania, and was completed in 1859, named for the man doing this drilling, Edwin Drake—hired by a group of businessmen for the project.

drawworks *n*: the hoisting mechanism on a drilling rig. It is a large winch that spools off or takes in the drilling line and thus raises or lowers the traveling block, the drill stem, and the bit.

drill ahead *v*: to continue drilling operations.

drill collar *n*: a heavy, thick-walled tube, usually steel, placed between the drill pipe and the bit in the drill stem. Several drill collars are used to apply weight on the bit.

driller *n*: the employee (of an independent or major company) directly in charge of a drilling rig and crew whole main duty is operation of the drilling and hoisting equipment. The driller is also responsible for the condition of the well and the supervision of the drilling crew.

drilling contractor *n*: an individual or group who owns a drilling rig or rigs and contracts services for drilling wells.

drill crew *n*: a driller, a derrickhand, and two or more floorhands. The minimum necessary workers to effectively make a well.

drilling engineer *n*: an engineer who specializes in the technical aspects of drilling.

drill fluid *n*: circulating fluid, one function of which is to lift cuttings out of the wellbore and to the surface. Other functions are to cool and lubricate the bit and the drill string and to offset the downhole formation pressures. Drilling fluids can be air, natural gas, foam, water, water and clay mud mixtures or even diesel, or synthetic oil types. See *mud*.

drilling rate *n*: the speed with which the bit drills the formation; usually called Rate of Penetration (ROP).

drill pipe *n*: jointed steel pipe made up in the drill stem between the Kelly or top drive on the surface and the bottomhole assembly at bottom. Joints are screwed together to form the drill string.

drill stem *n*: all components in the assembly used for rotary drilling from the swivel to the bit, including the kelly, the drill pipe, the drill collars, the stabilizers, and various specialty items. Compare *drill string*.

E

electric log *n*: an electrical survey made of certain electrical characteristics to identify the formations, determine the nature and amount of fluids contained underground, and an estimated depth.

electric rig *n*: a drilling rig usually with several diesel engines where the energy is changed from DC to AC electricity by generators. The AC is changed to an appropriate voltage of DC power in the control house. The correct voltage of DC current is sent from the control house to DC motors used to keep the rig alive—such as the drawworks or the pumps. Compare *mechanical rig*.

exploration *n*: the search for reservoirs of oil and gas, including aerial and geophysical surveys, geological studies, core testing, and wildcat drilling.

exploration well *n*: a well drilled either in search of an as-yet discovered pool or oil or gas (wildcatting); or to greatly extend the limits of a known poor—also known as a *step-out* well.

F

fastline *n*: the end of the drilling line that is affixed to the drum or reel of the drawworks. It travels with greater velocity than any other portion of the line as it is spooled or unspooled from the drawworks drum. Compare *deadline*.

fault *n*: a break in the Earth's crust along which rocks on one side have been displaced (up, down or sideways) relative to those on the other side.

field *n*: a geographical area in which a number of oil or gas wells produce from a continuous reservoir. A field may refer to surface area only or to underground productive formations. See *oilfield*.

fingerboard *n*: a rack that appears as a series of "fingers" with spaces in between the fingers. It supports the tops of the stands of pipe being stacked or "racked back" in the derrick or mast.

fish *n*: an object left in a wellbore during operations that must be recovered before work can proceed. Getting to the object is called simply "fishing." More commonly, these items include a lost bit, a drill collar, or even part of the drill pipe string.

fishermen *n pl*: experts in recovering objects lost in a well.

flare *v*: the act of burning a flow of hydrocarbons, such as a flowing gas stream.

floorhand *n*: a worker on a drilling or workover rig, subordinate to the driller and the derrickhand, whose primary work station is on the rig floor. Also called a rotary helper, floorman, rig crewman, or roughneck.

formation *n*: a bed composed of basically the same kind of rock. Formations are named by formation outcrops at surface and sometimes based on fossils the deposit contains.

formation fracturing *n*: a method of stimulating production by opening new flow channels in the rock surrounding a production well. Often called a "fracking" or a frac job. A fracturing fluid (water, oil, diesel, or acid) is pumped into a formation at a high enough pressure so that the rock cracks open forming a fracture. The fracture can be extended by continued high pressure injection of the fluid into the formation. The fracture is filled with material to hold the facture open when the pressure is removed. This material, called proppant, can be sand or any number of other materials. If the rock is a carbonate, like limestone, acid can be used to etch pathways along the fracture face. When the pressure is released at the surface, the fracturing fluid returns to the well and the fracture closes partially on the proppant or etched channels. The propped fracture provides a high permeability pathway for reservoir fluids flowing to the wellbore. Also called *fracturing*.

G

gamma ray log *n:* a device that measures the amount of naturally occurring gamma ray emissions from a formation. This is an indicator of the radioactive material content of the rock. The log is most frequently used as an indication of the shale or clay content of a formation.

geologist *n:* a scientist who gathers and interprets data pertaining to the rocks of the Earth's crust.

geology *n:* the science of the physical history of the Earth and its life, especially as recorded in rocks throughout the planetary crust.

geophysicist *n:* one who studies the way sound energy travels through the layers of the earth. The reflections of sound energy from the layers of rock in the earth can be interpreted as the buried structures that might trap oil and gas.

gooseneck *n*: the curved connection between the rotary hose and the swivel.

gusher *n*: (slang) an oilwell that has come in with such great pressure that the crude oil jets out of the well like a geyser. But a "gusher" is just a blowout and a big waste of natural resources. Rigs have made vast improvements to prevent such problems.

H

HCL *abbr*; hydrochloric acid.

HFL *abbr.* hydrofluoric acid.

hoist *n*: an arrangement of pulleys and wire rope or chain used for lifting heavy objects; a winch or similar device. 2. The drawworks. *v:* to raise or lift.

hole *n*: in drilling operations, the wellbore or borehole.

hook *n*: a large, hook-shaped device from which the swivel is suspended. It is designed to carry max loads ranging from 100 tons to 650 tons and turns on bearings in its supporting housing.

hook load *n*: the weight of the drill stem that is suspended from the hook.

horizontal drilling *n*: deviation of the vertical hole to 90-percent horizontal.

horsepower *n*: a unit of measure of work done by a machine. One horsepower equals 33,000 foot-pounds per minute.

hot wire *n*: heated filament that is used to combust small amounts of natural gas recovered from the drilling mud. The resulting heat can be calibrated as gas units which are a direct indication of natural gas in the well.

hydraulic *adj.* 1. Of or relating to water, or other fluid, in a state of movement. 2. Operated, moved, or affected by water or other fluid.

hydraulic jars *n:* a drilling tool that can be placed in the drill string and used to deliver a blow or shock to the drill string. The tool has a hydraulic piston inside that can be compressed or cocked by the correct movement of the drill string. The cocked piston can be released driving an internal hammer against an anvil. The impact creates a very strong force that acts along the drill string that can be directed either upward or downward. This force can help free a stuck drill string.

hydrocarbons *n.* pl. organic compounds of hydrogen and carbon whose densities, boiling points, and freezing points increase as their molecular weights increase. Although composed of only two elements, hydrocarbons exist in a variety of compounds because of the strong affinity of carbon atoms for other atoms and for itself. Petroleum is a mix of different hydrocarbons.

hydrochloric acid (HCL) *n:* an aqueous solution of hydrogen chloride; a strongly corrosive acid used mainly for dissolving limestone.

hydrocyclone *n:* a cone that develops centrifugal force when fluids are pumped through it. The centrifugal force is used to separate solids, like sand and silt, from the drilling mud.

hydrofluoric acid (HFL) *n:* a colorless, very corrosive acid that dissolves clay and sandstone.

hydrogas *n:* another term for liquefied petroleum gas (LPG).

hydrogen sulfide *n:* a compound of two hydrogen atoms bonded with one sulfur atom. This is a gas that can be a contaminant in oil and natural gas. Hydrogen sulfide is a poisonous gas and can be lethal at concentrations above 150 ppm. At very low concentrations around oilfields and rigs the gas has a rotten egg smell. At high concentrations the gas is odorless because it kills the sense of smell. A person or animal just passes out and dies without help.

IADC *abbr*: International Association of Drilling Contractors *n*: an organization of drilling contractors that sponsors or conducts research on education, accident prevention, drilling technology, and other matters of interest to drilling contractors and their employees. www. Iadc.org.

impermeable *adj*: not allowing the passage of fluid.

inclination *n:* the angle of the borehole from vertical. Measured in degrees with vertical being zero and horizontal being 90-degrees.

independent operator *n:* a nonintegrated oil company or an individual whose operations are in the field of petroleum production, excluding transportation, refining, and marketing. Major operators, big companies, take care of transporting, refining and marketing.

infill drilling *n:* drilling wells between known producing wells to exploit the resources of a field to best productive advantage.

inland barge *n:* floating drilling structure consisting of a barge on which drill equipment is constructed which can be transported where needed. When stationed on the drill site, the barge can be anchored in the floating mode or submerged to rest on the bottom, Typically, inland barge rigs are used to drill wells in marshes, shallow inland bays, and areas where the water is shallow. Also called a swamp barge.

insert *n:* cylindrical object, rounded, blunt, or chisel-shaped on one end and usually made of tungsten carbide, that is inserted in the cones of a bit, the cutters of a reamer, or the blades of a stabilizer to form the cutting element of the bit or the reamer or the wear surface of the stabilizer. Also called a compact.

intermediate casing *n*: the string of casing set in a well after the surface casing but before production casing is set to keep the hole from caving and to seal off troublesome formations. In deep wells, one or more intermediate strings may be required. Also called protection casing.

Iron Roughneck (Trademark) *n*: a manufacturer's name for a floor-mounted combination of a spinning wrench and a torque wrench. Iron Roughneck ™ moves into position hydraulically and eliminates the manual handling involved with making up or breaking out pipe. This is a "power tong" function. Take the "power" away and this is hard manual labor with a tong.

J

jet *n*: 1. a hydraulic device operated by a centrifugal pump used to clean the mud pits, or tanks, and to mix mud components. 2. In a perforating gun using shaped charges, a highly penetrating, fast-moving stream of exploded particles that forms a hole in the casing, cement, and formation. 3. Nozzle in a bit.

jetted *v*: the act of pumping waste fluids from one pit to another. A common practice where shale and reserve pits are used.

joint *n*: a single length (from 16 feet to 45 feet, or 5 meters to 14.5 meters) of drill pipe, drill collar, casing, or tubing that has threaded connections at both ends.

junk mills *n pl*: a drag bit that has tungsten carbide as a cutting structure. The very hard tungsten carbide can drill away or mill down pieces of metal that lodged or were left in the well as junk.

K

kelly *n*: the heavy steel tubular device, four-or-six-sided, suspended from the swivel through the rotary table and connected to the top joint of drill pipe to turn the drill stem as the rotary table turns. It has a bored passageway that permits fluid to be circulated into the drill stem and up the annulus.

kelly drive bushing *n*: a device that fits into the master bushing of the rotary table and through which the kelly runs. When the master bushing rotates the kelly drive bushing, the Kelly drive bushing rotates the Kelly and the drill stem attached to the Kelly.

kelly spinner *n*: a pneumatically operated device mounted on top of the Kelly that, when powered, causes the Kelly to turn, or spin. It is used when making up or breaking out the Kelly from the drill string.

kerogen *n:* the organic source of hydrocarbons.

kick *n*: an entry of water, gas, oil, or combination of those fluids into the wellbore during drilling. It occurs because the pressure exerted by the column of drilling fluid is not great enough to overcome the pressure from the drilled formation fluids.

kilometers *n*: a unit of length of distance in the metric and SI units systems. One kilometer equals 1,000 meters, or 3,280.84 feet.

L

land rig *n:* any drilling rig that is located on dry land. Compare *offshore rig, or swamp barge.*

latch on *v*: to attach elevators to a section of pipe to pull it out of or run into the hole.

lead tongs *n pl*: pipe tongs (screws or unscrews) suspended in the derrick or mast and operated by a chain or wire rope connected to the makeup cathead or the breakout cathead. See makeup tongs.

lease *n*: an agreement that gives the petroleum prospector the right to explore land for oil, gas, and sometimes other minerals and to extract them from the ground. If the landowner has legal mineral rights, the drilling company pays a percentage of the profits from production.

limestone *n*: an evaporite mineral (rock) type made up of calcium carbonate ($CaCO_3$).

liner *n*: a string of pipe used to case open hole below existing casing. A liner extends from the setting depth up into another string of casing, usually overlapping about 100 feet (30 meters) into the upper string.

liquefied natural gas (LNG) *n*: a natural gas that has been cooled to minus 260-degrees Fahrenheit at atmospheric pressure. At this very cold temperature, the has becomes a liquid. If allowed to return to a normal temperature the liquid vaporizes. LNG occupies about 1/600th of the volume it occupied as a gas and the liquid can be shipped in safe, insulated containers.

liquefied petroleum gas (LPG) *n*: a propane or butane gas that has been pressurized to the point where it turns into a liquid. LPG must be stored and shipped in pressurized containers. If the pressure is released, the liquid propane or butane vaporizes. See hydrogas.

liquid *n*: a state of matter in which the shape of the given mass depends on the containing vessel, but the volume of the mass is independent of the vessel. A liquid is a fluid that is almost incompressible.

log *n:* a systematic recording of data, such as a driller's log, a mud log, an electrical well log, or a nuclear log. v: to record data.

logging while drilling (LWD) *n*: logging measurements obtained using techniques while the well is being drilled.

M

magnetometer *n*: a device that measures the strength of the Earth's magnetic field. Used in directional drilling to determine the compass bearing of the well bottom.

major *n*: a large oil company, such as ExxonMobil or Chevron, that not only produces oil, but also transports, refines, and markets petroleum and its products.

make a connection *v*: to attach a joint of drill pipe onto the drill stem suspended in the wellbore to permit deepening the wellbore by the length of the joint (normally about 30 feet, or nine meters.)

make up *v*: to assemble and join parts to form a complete unit (such as: to make up a string of casing). 2. To screw together two threaded pieces. 3. To mix or prepare (such as a tank of mud).

makeup cathead *n*: a device that is attached to the shaft of the drawworks and used as a power source for screwing together joints of pipe. It is the automatic cathead located on the driller's side of the drawworks. See cathead. Compare breakout cathead.

makeup tongs *n pl*: tongs used for screwing one length of pipe into another for making up a joint. See lead tongs, tongs.

making hole *v*: to deepen the hole made by the bit, and to drill ahead.

male connection *n*: a pipe, a coupling, or a tool that has threads on the outside so that it can be joined to the threads on the inside of a female connection. Also called the pin. Compare to female connection.

manifold *n*: an accessory system of piping to a main piping system (or another conductor) that serves to divide a flow into several parts, to combine several flows into one, or to reroute a flow to any one of several possible destinations.

mast *n*: a portable derrick that is capable of being raised as a unit. Compare derrick.

master bushing *n*: a device that fits into the rotary table to accommodate the slips and drive the Kelly bushing so that the rotating motion of the rotary table can be transmitted to the kelly. Also called rotary bushing.

matrix *n*: the shape of the bit.

measurement while drilling (MWD) *n*: directional or other surveying during routine drilling operations to determine the angle and direction by which the wellbore deviates from vertical. The measured data are encoded and transmitted to the surface recorder as a series of pressure pulses in the mud. The surface recorder sends the code to a computer where it is converted back into the measured data. 2. Any system of measuring and transmitting to the surface downhole information during routine drilling operations. See logging while drilling.

mechanical rig *n*: a drilling rig in which the source of power is one of more internal-combustion engines and in which the power is distributed to the rig components through mechanical devices (such as chains, sprockets, clutches, and shafts). Also called a power rig. Compare electric rig.

methane *n*: the simplest hydrocarbon compound. Methane is an odorless and colorless gas made up of four hydrogen atoms bonded to a single carbon atom (CH4). Methane is the largest single component by volume in natural gas.

meter *n*: the fundamental unit of length in the international system of measurement (SI). It is equal to about 3.28 feet, 39.37 inches, or 100 centimeters.

metric ton *n*: a measurement of mass equal to 1,000 kilograms or 2,204.6 pounds. In some oil-producing countries, production is reported in metric tons. One metric ton is equal to about 7.4 barrels (42 U.S. gallons equal to one barrel) of crude oil, but this depends on the density of the oil. In the SI system it is called a tonne.

mill *n*: a downhole drag bit with rough, sharp, extremely hard tungsten carbide cutting surfaces for removing metals by grinding or cutting. They are also called junk mills or reaming mills depending on usage, v: to use a mill to cut or grind out metal objects that must be removed from a well.

mineral rights n pl: the rights of ownership, conveyed by deed, of gas, oil, or any type of minerals located subsurface. In the U.S., mineral rights are the property of the surface owner unless disposed of separately. In most other countries the mineral rights are state property. Dictators often seize funds from state-owned mineral rights.

monkeyboard *n*: the derrickhand's working platform at the correct height in the derrick for handling the top of the pipe. As the pipe is run into or out of the hole, the derrickman must handle the top end of the pipe (90 feet—or 27 meters—or higher in the mast, also known as the derrick.

mousehole *n*: an opening through the rig floor, usually lined with pipe, into which a length of drill pipe is placed temporarily for later connection to the drill string.

mud *n*: the liquid circulated through the wellbore during rotary drilling operations. In addition to its function of bringing cuttings to the surface, drilling mud cools and lubricates the bit and the drill stem, protects against blowouts by holding back subsurface pressures, and deposits a mud cake on the wall of the borehole to prevent loss of fluids to the formation. See drilling fluid.

mud centrifuge *n*: a device that uses centrifugal force to separate small solid components from liquid drilling fluid.

mud engineer *n*: an employee of a drilling fluid supply company whose duty it is to test and maintain the drilling mud properties that are specified by the operator.

mud logging *n*: the recording of information derived from examination and analysis of formation cuttings made by the bit, and of mud circulated out of the hole.

mud pit *n:* originally, an open pit dug in the ground to hold drilling fluid or waste materials discarded after the treatment of drilling mud. For some drilling operations, mud pits are used for suction to the mud pumps, settling of drilled cuttings, and storage of reserve mud. Steel tanks are commonly used now but still referred to as pits. Offshore, the term "mud tanks" is common.

mud pump *n:* a large, high-pressure positive displacement pump used to circulate the mud on a drilling rig. Also called a slush pump.

mud return line *n:* a trough or pipe placed between surface connections at the wellbore through which drilling mud flows after returning to the surface from the well hole. Also called a flow line.

mud weight *n:* a measure of the density of a drilling fluid expressed as pounds per gallon, pounds per cubic foot, or kilograms per cubic meter. Mud weight is directly related to the amount of pressure the column of drilling mud exerts at the bottom of the hole.

mule shoe *n:* a cut lip on the overshot that acts as a guide and allows the overshot to be rotated over the fish. (Explain).

N

natural gas *n:* a highly compressible, highly expandable mixture of hydrocarbons with a low specific gravity and occurring naturally in a gaseous form. Besides hydrocarbon gases, natural gas may contain appreciable quantities of nitrogen, helium, carbon dioxide, hydrogen sulfide, and water vapor.

neutron log *n:* a tool that can be used as an indirect indication of formation porosity. The log records the radioactive response from a formation to the bombardment of the formation with neutrons. The neutrons are slowed by collisions with large atoms like hydrogen. Hydrogen occurs in water, oil and gas that occur only in the pore space of the rock. The more hydrogen presents the faster the neutrons are slowed down and the larger the porosity is inferred to be. Unlike the density log, which also is a porosity indicator, the neutron log can be used to open holes and in wells that have been cased.

night toolpusher *n:* an assistant whose duty hours are typically during nighttime hours on a mobile offshore drilling unit.

nippled up *v*: 1. To assemble the blowout preventer (BOP) stack or other wellhead components on the wellhead at the surface. 2. To assemble.

nozzle *n*: a passageway through jet bits that causes the drilling fluid to be ejected from the bit at high velocity. The jets of mud clear the bottom of the hole and help keep the cutting structures of the bit clean.

O

off-bottom weight *n*: the weight of the drill string that is suspended by the derrick before the bit is allowed to touch well bottom.

offshore rig *n*: any of various types of drilling structures designed for use in drilling wells in oceans, seas, bays, gulfs, waterways or bayous. Offshore rigs oil *n*: a simple or complex liquid mixture of hydrocarbons that can be refined to yield gasoline, kerosene, diesel fuel, and a wide range of other products.

oilfield *n*: referring to an area where oil is found. May also include the oil reservoir, the surface and the wells, and production equipment.

oil seep *n*: a surface location where oil appears, the oil having permeated its subsurface boundaries and accumulated in small pools or rivulets. Also called an oil spring.

on-bottom weight *n*: the weight of the drill string suspended by the derrick after the bit has been allowed to touch the bottom of the well. The difference between the off-bottom and on-bottom weights is the weight that has been placed on the bit to make it drill.

open hole *n*: any wellbore in which casing has not been set.

open-hole fishing *n*: the procedure of recovering lost or stuck equipment in an uncased wellbore.

operator *n*: the person or company actually operating an oil well, that hired a drilling contractor. The term operator carries the connotation of authority over the well from beginning to end. The operator oversees all operations during the life of the well.

P

P & A *abbr:* plug and abandon.

PDC bit *n*: a special type of man-made diamond drag bit. Polycrystalline diamond inserts, or compacts, are embedded into a matrix on the bit.

perforate *v*: to pierce the casing wall and cement of a wellbore, providing holes through which formation fluids may enter or to provide holes in the casing or tubing so that materials may be introduced into the annulus.

perforating gun *n*: a device fitted with shaped charges or bullets that is lowered to the desired depth in a well and fired to create penetrating holes in casing, cement, and formation.

permeability *n*: 1. A measure of the ease with which a fluid flows through the connecting pore spaces of a rock. The unit of measurement is square meters. 2. Fluid conductivity of a porous medium. 3. Ability of fluid to flow within the interconnected pore network of a porous medium.

personal protective equipment (PPE) *n*: items issues to individuals at the rig site and used for the individual's personal protection. The items are safety glasses, hearing protection, a hard hat, steel-toed boots or shoes, special coveralls, face shields, gloves, and safety harnesses.

petrochemical feedstock *n*: hydrocarbons used as the basis for petrochemicals like pharmaceuticals, plastics, and synthetic rubber.

petroleum *n*: substance occurring naturally in the earth in solid (tar), liquid (crude oil), or gaseous (natural gas) state and composed mainly of mixtures of chemical compounds of carbon and hydrogen, with or without other nonmetallic elements such as sulfur, oxygen, and nitrogen. In some cases, especially in the measurement of oil and gas, petroleum refers only to oil—a liquid hydrocarbon—and does not include natural gas or gas liquids such as propane and butane. The American Petroleum Institute prefers that petroleum mean crude oil and not natural gas or gas liquids.

petroleum geology *n*: the study of oil-and-gas-bearing rock formations, dealing with the origin, occurrence, movement and accumulation of hydrocarbons.

pick up *v*: to use the drawworks to lift the bit (or other tool) off bottom by raising the drill stem. 2. to use an air hoist or friction cathead to lift a tool, a joint of drill pope, or other piece of equipment.

piercement salt dome *n*: a salt dome pushed up so that it penetrates the overlying sediments, leaving them scaled back.

pile driver *n*: a ram that is used like a large hammer to drive posts, piles, and conductor casing into the earth. The ram is attached to a hydraulic cylinder and driven by a power source like a diesel engine.

pipe rack *n*: a horizontal storage support. Pipe Racker: a pneumatic or hydraulic device that, on command from an operator, either picks up pipe from a rack or from the side of the derrick and lifts it into the derrick or takes pipe from out of the derrick and places it on the racks or places it to the side of the derrick. This machine takes the place of the derrickman and in some cases the floormen, as well.

pipe ram *n*: a sealing component for a blowout preventer that closes the annular space between the pipe and the blowout preventer or wellhead.

pipe tally *n:* a written or digital record of the individual dimensions (inner and outer diameter and length) of a string of pipe that has been placed in a well.

play *n*: 1. The extent of a petroleum-bearing formation. 2. The activities associated with petroleum development in an area.

plug and abandon *v:* to place cement and/or mechanical plugs into a dry hole or a depleted well to seal and abandon it.

pore *n:* an opening or space within a rock or mass of rocks, usually small and often filled with some fluid (water, oil, gas, or all three). Porosity: 1. the condition of being porous (such as a rock formation). 2. The ratio of the volume of empty space to the total (bulk) volume of rock in a formation, indicating how much fluid a rock formation can hold.

posted barge *n:* a submersible rig for shallow water or marsh locations. The rig has the drilling platform raised above a barge hull by steel posts. The rig is towed to location and the barge hull flooded and sunk to the bottom. The steel posts keep the rig floor above water.

pressure *n:* the force that a fluid (liquid or gas) exerts uniformly in all directions within a vessel, a pipe, a hole in the ground, etc., such as that exerted against the inner wall of a tank or that exerted on the bottom of a wellbore by a fluid. Pressure is expressed in terms of force exerted per unit of area, as pounds per square inch, or in kilopascals.

prime mover *n:* an internal combustion engine or a motor that is the source of power for driving a machine or machines.

production *n:* the part of the petroleum industry that deals with bringing the well fluids to the surface and separating them and with storing, gauging, and otherwise preparing the product for the pipeline. 2. The amount of oil or gas produced in a given period.

production casing *n:* the last string of casing set in a well, inside of which is usually suspected a tubing string.

production wellhead n: the control valves through which oil and/or natural gas are produced. See wellhead.

propping agent n: a granular substance (sand grains, bauxite, or other material) that is carried in suspension by the fracturing fluid and that serves to keep the cracks open when the fracturing pressure is released after a fracture treatment.

pulley n: a wheel with a grooved rim, used for pulling or hoisting. Also called a sheave.

pull line n: a length of wire rope, one end of which is connected to the end of the tongs and the other end connected to the chain on the automatic cathead on the drawworks. When the driller actuates the cathead, it takes in the tong line and exerts force on the tong to either make up or break out drill pipe.

pull singles *v*: to remove the drill stem from the hole by disconnecting each individual joint.

pump *n:* a device that increases the pressure of a liquid.

R

rack *n*: framework for supporting or containing drill pipe and related materials.

racked back *v*: the process of taking a stand of drill pipe or drill collars and placing the top inside the fingers of the fingerboard for temporary storage. The stands are placed one after another or racked back in the fingerboard.

ram *n*: the closing and sealing component on a blowout preventer. One of three types—blind, pipe, or shear—may be installed in several preventers mounted in a stack on top of a wellbore.

ram blowout preventer *n*: a blowout preventer that uses rams to seal off pressure on a hole that is with or without pipe. Also called ram preventer.

rate of penetration (ROP) *n*: a measure of the speed at which the bit drills into formations, usually expressed in feet (meters) per hour or minutes per foot or meter.

rathole *n*: a hole in the rig floor, which is lined with a pipe that projects above the floor and into which the kelly and swivel are placed when hoisting operations are in progress.

rathole rig *n:* a small, usually truck-mounted rig used to drill the rathole and the mousehole for the main drilling rig which will be moved in later. A rathole rig may also drill the top part of the hole, the conductor hole, before the main rig arrives on location.

repeat formation tester (RFT) *n*: a wireline conveyed formation evaluation tool that can obtain formation pressures and fluid samples from open-hole sections of the well.

reserve pit *n*: a waste pit, an excavated earthen-walled pit. It may be lined with plastic or other material to prevent soil contamination.

reservoir *n*: a subsurface, porous, permeable rock body in which oil or gas has accumulated. Reservoir rock: a permeable rock that may contain oil or gas in appreciable quantity through which fluids can migrate.

rig *n:* the derrick or mast, drawworks, and attendant surface equipment of a drilling unit.

rig floor *n*: the area immediately around the rotary table and extending to each corner of the derrick or mast. Also called derrick floor, drill floor.

rigging down *v*: 1. To dismantle a drilling rig and auxiliary equipment following the completion of drilling operations. Also called tear down. 2. In general, to disassemble.

rigging up *v*: 1. To prepare the drilling rig for making hole—to install tools and machinery before drilling is started.

rig hand *n*: a crewmember who is part of a drilling crew. See derrickman, driller, floorhand.

rig manager *n:* an employee of a drilling contractor who is in charge of the entire drilling crew and the drilling rig, providing logistics support to the rig crew and liaison with the operating company. See *toolpusher*.

rock *n:* a hardened aggregate of different minerals. Rocks are divided into three groups on the basis of their mode of origin: igneous, metamorphic, and sedimentary.

roller cone *n:* a drill bit made of three cones that are mounted on rugged bearings. The surface of each cone has rows of steel teeth or rows of tungsten carbide inserts. When the bit is rotated, the cones roll across the rock surface. This action causes the teeth on the cones to first crush and then shear rock into fragments or cuttings. Also called rock bits.

rotary *n:* the machine used to impart rotational power to the kelly and drill stem while permitting vertical movement of the pipe for rotary drilling.

rotary drilling *n:* a drilling method in which a hole is drilled by a rotating bit to which a downward force is applied. The bit is fastened to and rotated by the drill stem, which also provides a passageway through which the drilling fluid is circulated.

rotary rig *n:* a drilling rig system of rotating a bit while also circulating fluid through the drill pipe during drilling operations.

rotary steerable assembly *n:* a directional drilling tool that allows the path of the wellbore to be measured and the position changed while rotating the drill string.

rotary table *n:* the principal component of a rotary, or rotary machine, used to turn the drill stem and support the drilling assembly.

rotary-table system *n:* a series of devices that provide a way to rotate the drill stem and bit. Basic components consist of a turntable, master bushing, kelly drive bushing, a kelly, and a swivel.

rotating head *n*: a device that is placed on top of the drilling wellhead that seals the wellbore while still allowing the drill string to be rotated. A rotating head resembles an Annular Blowout Preventer except that the sealing element has a bearing that allows it to rotate.

rotor *n*: the rotating inner shaft of a motor. The inner shaft rotates inside a fixed housing caked the stator. The rotor is caused to turn inside the stator by applied force. In the case of an electric motor, the force is created by the electric current flowing through the stator. In the case of a drilling motor, it is created by the pressure from the drilling mud that is pumped through the motor.

round trip *n*: the action of pulling out and subsequently running back into the hole a string of drill pipe or tubing. Also called tripping.

roustabout *n*: a worker on a rig responsible for odd jobs or to pitch in upon request by a fellow crewman. Roustabouts can also handle equipment and supplies. A head roustabout is usually the crane operator.

royalty *n*: a share of the money made from the sale of oil or gas that is paid to the mineral owner.

run casing *v*: to lower a string of casing into the hole. Also called to run pipe.

run in *v*: to go into the hole with tubing, drill pipe, and other equipment.

running quicksand *n*: extremely unconsolidated sand that will not hold its shape when drilled. The loose sand caves in quickly filling the hole.

S

safety slide *n*: a wireline device normally mounted near the monkeyboard to afford the derrickman a means of quick exit to the surface in case of emergency. It is usually affixed to the wireline, one end of which is attached to the derrick or mast and the other end to the surface. To exit the safety slide. The derrickman grasps a handle on it and rides it down to the ground. Also called Geronimo or the Tinkerbell Line.

salt dome *n*: a dome that is caused by an intrusion of salt into overlying sediments. See *piercement salt dome*.

samples *n pl*: 1. the well cuttings obtained at designated footage intervals during drilling. From an examination of these cuttings, the geologist determines the type of rock formations being drilled and estimates oil and gas content. 2. Small quantities of well fluids obtained for analysis.

sand *n:* 1. an abrasive material composed of small quartz grains formed from the disintegration of pre-existing rocks. Sand consists of particles less than .078 inch. 2. Sandstone.

sand reel *n:* a winch. A drum, operated by a wheel, for raising or lowering the sand pump or bailer during drilling.

scratcher *n*: a device that is fastened to the outside of casing to remove mud cake from the wall of a hole to condition the hole for cementing. By rotating or moving the casing string up and down as it is being tun into the hole, the scratcher, formed of still wire, removes the cake so the cement can bond hard to the formation.

SCR house *n*: the control house where the AC Current is converted to DC current and transmitted to the various motors on the rig. SCR stands for the AC to DC conversion process known as silicon-controlled rectification.

seafloor *n*: the bottom of the ocean. The seabed.

seat *n*: the point in the wellbore at which the bottom of the casing is set.

seep *n*: the surface appearance of oil or gas that results naturally when a reservoir-rock becomes exposed to the surface, thus allowing oil or gas to flow out of fissures in the rock.

seismic *adj:* of or relating to an earthquake or earth vibration, including those artificially induced.

seismic survey *n:* an exploration method in which strong low-frequency sound waves are generated on the surface or in the water and reflect off sub-surface rocks possibly containing hydrocarbons. Interpretation of the record can reveal possible oil and gas bearing formations.

self-elevating substructure *n:* a base on which the floor and mast of a drilling rig rests and which, after it is placed in the desired location, is raised into position as a single unit, normally using hydraulic pistons.

semisubmersible *n:* a floating offshore drilling unit that has pontoons and columns that, when flooded, cause the unit to submerge to a predetermined depth. Semisubmersibles are more stable than drillships and use used extensively to drill wildcat wells in rough waters such as in the North Sea. *See floating offshore rig.*

set back *v:* to place stands of drill pipe and drill collars in a vertical position to one side of the rotary table in the fingerboard of the derrick or mast or a drilling or workover rig. *See racked back.*

shale *n:* a fine-grained sedimentary rock composed mostly of consolidated clay or mud. Shale is the most frequently occurring sedimentary rock. *See shale pit.*

shale shaker *n:* a vibrating screen used to remove cuttings from the circulating fluid in rotary drilling operations. The size of the openings in the screen should be carefully selected to be the smallest size possible to allow 100 percent flow of the fluid through the screen. Also called *shaker.*

shaped charge *n:* a relatively small conical shaped container of high explosive loaded into a perforating gun, on detonation, the charge releases a small, high-velocity stream of particles (a jet) that penetrates the casing, cement and formation *See perforating gun.*

shear ram *n*: the component in a blowout preventer that cuts, or shears, through drill pipe and forms a seal against well pressure.

shut in *v*: 1. to close the valves on a well so that it stops producing. 2. To close in a well in which a kick has occurred.

sidewall core *n*: a small cylindrical rock sample (about one-inch by three-inches) obtained using an electric wireline conveyed sidewall core gun. The sample is extracted by driving a core barrel into the wide of the borehole wall and then pulling the barrel with the sample out.

sidewall core gun *n*: a device run into the well on an electric wireline. The gun has twenty-five empty core barrels loaded in front with explosive charges. The barrels are connected to the gun with steel cables. Once positioned to the correct depth, individual core barrels are fired into the side of the hole and a sample is retrieved when the gun is moved. Sidewall core guns can be run in tandem to recover fifty or more samples per run into the well.

single *n:* a joint of drill pipe. *Compare double, triple, quadruple.*

sinker bar *n*: a heavy weight or bar placed on or near a lightweight wireline tool. The bar provides the weight so that the tool will lower properly into the well.

skid the rig *v*: to drag parts of the rig to a new location.

SL *abbr:* surface location.

slack off *v*: to let go of tension on the drill string.

side-drilling *n*: a process in which the direction of the bottom of the well is changed. The method used a bent housing motor where the bit can be pointed in a new direction. The bit is rotated by the motor, but the drill string is not rotated. The bit drills in the new direction with the drill string sliding along behind.

slips *n pl:* wedge-shaped pieces of metal with teeth or other gripping elements that are used to prevent pipe from slipping down into a hole or to hold pipe into place.

slurry *n:* in drilling, a plastic mix of cement and water that is pumped into a well to harden. There it supports the casing and provides a seal in the wellbore to prevent migration of underground fluids.

sonic log *n:* a wireline tool that provides an indication of formation porosity. The tool measures the time required for sounds to travel from a transmitter on the tool through the formation and back to the tool. The time required to travel this fixed distance is proportional to the volume and type of rock and the volume and type of fluid present in the formation.

sour crude *n:* oil containing hydrogen sulfide gas. A deadly oilfield element that smells like rotten eggs at low levels, but kills at higher levels·by destroying sense of smell. The victim dies fairly soon—especially while asleep.

spear *n:* a fishing tool used to retrieve pipe lost in a well. The spear is lowered down the hole and into the lost pipe. When weight, torque, or both are applied to the string to which the spear is attached, the slips in the spear expand and tightly grip the inside of the wall in the lost pipe.

Spindletop *n:* the name of the location of the 1901 Lucas gusher near Beaumont, Texas. This famous well demonstrated that vast quantities of oil could be found and produced from a drilled well and that rotary drilling technology was superior to cable-tool technology.

spinning wrench *n:* air-powered or hydraulically powered wrench used to spin drill pipe when making up or breaking connections.

spool *n:* the drawworks drum. Also, a casinghead or drilling spool. v: to wind around a drum. Slang: *"Wind up your spool. You're fired."*

spudded *v:* to begin drilling. To start the hole.

SSV *abbr:* surface safety valve.

SSSV *abbr:* subsurface safety valve.

stab *v:* to guide the end of a pipe into a coupling or tool joint when making up a connection.

stabilizer *n:* a tool placed on a drill collar near the bit that is used, depending on where it is placed, either to maintain a particular hole handle or to change the angle by controlling the location of the contact point between the hole and other collars.

stand *n:* the connected joints of a pipe racked in the derrick or mast when making a trip. On a rig, the usual stand is about 90 feet long—three lengths of pipe together. Or a *triple.*

standard derrick *n:* built piece by piece at the drill location. Compare to *mast.*

standpipe *n:* a vertical pipe rising along the side of the derrick or mast, which joins the discharge line leading from the mud pump to the rotary hose and through which mud is pumped into the hole.

stimulate *v:* the action of attempting to improve and enhance a well's performance by creating factures in the rock, or using chemicals such as acid to dissolve part of the rocks and remove fluid contained. *See enhanced recovery.*

Subsurface Safety Valve (SSSV) *n:* a device installed in the tubing string of a producing well to shut in the flow of production if the pressure in the control line drops. The valve is placed in the tubing below either ground level or the mud line.

supply reel *n:* a spool that holds extra drilling line.

surface casing *n*: the first string of casing (after the conductor pipe) that is set in a well. It varies in length from a few hundred to several thousand feet. Some states require minimum length to protect freshwater sands.

surface hole *n*: that part of the wellbore that is drilled below the conductor hole but above the intermediate hole. Surface casing is run and cemented in the surface hole.

Surface Safety Valve (SSV) *n*: a valve, mounted in the Christmas Tree assembly, the stops the flow of fluids from the well in response to sensors.

swamp barge *n*: see inland barge.

swamper *n*: (slang) a helper on a truck, tractor, or other machine.

sweet crude *n:* oil containing little or no sulfur, especially with little to no hydrogen sulfide.

swivel *n:* a rotary tool hung from the rotary hook and the traveling block to suspend the drill stem and to permit it to rotate freely. It also provides a connection for the rotary hose and a passage for the flow of drilling fluid into the drill stem.

T

tally *v:* to measure and record the total length of pipe, casing, or tubing that is to be run in a well one joint at a time.

tap *v:* to bore a hole.

TD *abbr.* total depth.

Tectonic plate *n:* a massive, irregularly shaped slab of solid rock on the Earth's crust, generally composed of both continental and oceanic lithosphere which moves.

thermally stable polycrystalline (TSP) diamond bit *n*: a special type of drag bit that has synthetic diamond cutters that do not disintegrate at high temperatures and pressures.

thumper *n*: a truck used in seismic surveys that creates the energy pulse necessary by hitting or vibrating the ground with a hydraulic ram.

tongs *n pl*: the large wrenches used to make up o break out drill pipe, casing, tubing, or other pipe; variously called casing tongs, pipe tongs, and so forth, according to specific uses.

tool joint *n:* a heavy coupling element for drill pipe.

toolpush *n*: Canadian term for "toolpusher".

top drive *n*: a device similar to a power swivel that is used in place of the rotary table to turn the drill stem. Hung from a hook on the traveling block, a top drive also suspends the drill stem in the hole and includes pipe elevators. The top drive is powered by a motor or motors and includes a swivel.

top plug *n*: a cement plug that follows cement slurry down the casing. It goes before the fluid used to displace the cement from the casing and separates the displacement fluid from the slurry.

topside *n*: the deck placed above water and land on drilling and production platforms.

tour *n*: a working shift for drilling crew members or other oilfield workers. One rigs where tours are eight hours, the are called daylight, afternoon/ night and morning. Sometimes 12-hour tours are called-for, especially with offshore teams. These are known as the day or night tours.

transmission *n:* the gear or chain arrangement by which power is transmitted from the prime mover to the drawworks, the mud pump, or the rotary table of the rig.

trap *n:* a body of permeable oil-bearing rock surrounded or overlain by an impermeable barrier that prevents oil from escaping. The types of traps are structural, stratigraphic, or a combination. See fault trap.

traveling block *n:* an arrangement of pulleys, or sheaves, through which drilling line is strung and which moved up and down in the derrick or mast. *See block.*

trim *n:* the type of material used in wellhead control valves and chokes. For example: a valve made of stainless steel will have a stainless-steel trim. v: to cut short pieces from an object.

trip *n:* the operation of hoisting the drill stem from and returning it to the wellbore. Shortened form of *making a trip.*

tripping in and tripping out *v:* to lower and raise the drill stem into and out of the wellbore.

tungsten carbine bit *n:* a type or roller cone bit with inserts made of tungsten carbide. Extremely hard material.

turnkey contract *n:* a drilling contract that calls for the payment of a stipulated amount to the drilling contractor on completion of the well. In a turnkey contract, the contractor furnishes all materials and labor and controls the whole operation. He is independent of outside drilling supervision. A turnkey contract does not mean the contractor will having any part in production—though it happens. Those men made all kinds of deals.

V

value moment *n:* more commonly called a safety moment or meeting. A meeting held before the start of a new job where the job process and duties of the people involved are reviewed. Amy potential hazards are pointed out and remedies discussed. Additionally, the relevance or importance of the job to the outcome of the project is discussed.

V-door *n*: an opening at floor level of a derrick or mast shaped like an inverted V. The V-door is used as an entry to bring in drill pipe, casing and other tools from the pipe rack.

W

waiting on cement (WOC) *adj*: pertaining to the time when drilling or completion operations are suspended so that the cement in a well can harden sufficiently.

walking beam *n*: the large steel or wooden beam that connects the power end of a cable-tool rig to the cable that suspended the bit from the well. The beam is suspended above the ground on a steel or wooden A-shaped frame called the Sampson Post. The walking beam is moved up and down by the power section of the right which causes the bit on the cable to move up and down in the well striking rock on the bottom in order to keep making hole. However slowly.

wall cake *n*: a lining of clay particles that form over the face of permeable formations that are drilled in a well if water-base drilling mud is being used. The clay lining restricts the loss from liquid from the drilling mud into the formation and acts as a stabilizing sheath over the formation.

weight indicator *n*: an instrument near the driller's position on a drilling rig that show both the weight of the drill steam that is hanging from the hook (hook load) and the weight that is placed on the bit by the drill collars (weight on bit).

well completion *n*: a. the methods of preparing a well for the production of oil and gas or for other purposes, such as injection; the method for which one or more flow paths for hydrocarbons are established between the reservoir and the surface. 2. The system of tubulars, packers, and other tools installed beneath the wellhead in the production casing—this is the tool assembly that provides the hydrocarbon flow path or pathways.

Index

A

Alfred Flournoy M.D.
    Alfred Flournoy, M.D., xii, 135
Alice, Texas 28, 60, 73, 113

B

Betty Louise "Boo" Fields" 114
Bill Mason 7
Black Giant 1, 95

C

Camp Flournoy 34, 137, 138, 139
Colonel Cole 10

D

DeOrsay Simpson 30, 41
Duncan Chisholm 151

E

Evelyn Flournoy 120
ExxonMobil 64, 194

F

Fidel Rul 85, 86, 90
Flournoy Drilling Company 64, 66, 96, 99

G

Gene Kranz 84, 87
George Parr 6, 142, 144
Greenwood, Louisiana 3, 128

H

House Speaker Sam Rayburn 68

J

Jackie Richardson 115
Jane McClurg 44
Jean Carson 116, 147
Jim Wells County Commissioner
    Lawrence Cornelius 161

K

King Ranch 6, 22, 33, 64, 115, 116, 157

L

Linnie Key 154, 157
Lucien Flournoy xiii, xix, 3, 4, 9, 11, 27, 34, 52, 60, 62, 69, 99, 113, 117, 119, 121, 122, 124, 133, 137
Lucien Flournoy Sr. 11, 34

M

Magnolia Ranch 115
Marmalade (second rig) 25
Medical School xiv, xvii
Mississippi River 130

N

Natchitoches xvii, 3, 32, 33, 134
New Orleans v, xv, xvi, xvii, 3, 19, 33,
    125, 129, 130, 139

O

Old Bread and Butter (first rig) 25,
    33, 114

P

Pete Peterson 66
Pump Jack 40

R

Red River xix, 128, 130, 133
Red West 66, 93
Rheumatoid Arthritis 22, 119, 121

Rodessa Fields 1

S

Sam Flournoy 124
Sheriff J. Howell Flournoy 48
Shreveport 23, 26, 31, 34, 35, 36, 38,
    49, 50, 51, 113, 114, 128, 129,
    131, 133, 134, 139, 149
Shriner's Hospital 22
Silas Flournoy xiii, 138
Sue Murdoch 101

T

Texas Gov. Mark White 133

W

War of 1812 xii, 125
WASP 26, 28, 69, 70, 72, 73, 74, 75,
    76, 77, 78, 79, 80, 81, 82, 83, 84
W. Carlton "Tubby" Weaver 54

Y

Youree Hamilton 37